life
in a northern town

life
in a northern town

COOKING, EATING, AND OTHER ADVENTURES ALONG LAKE SUPERIOR

MARY DOUGHERTY

WISCONSIN HISTORICAL SOCIETY PRESS

Published by the Wisconsin Historical Society Press
Publishers since 1855

The Wisconsin Historical Society helps people connect to the past
by collecting, preserving, and sharing stories. Founded in 1846,
the Society is one of the nation's finest historical institutions.
Order books by phone toll free: (888) 999-1669
Order books online: shop.wisconsinhistory.org
Join the Wisconsin Historical Society: wisconsinhistory.org/membership

Printed in Canada
Designed by Brian Donahue / bedesign, inc.

21 20 19 18 17   1 2 3 4 5

Library of Congress Cataloging-in-Publication Data applied for.

∞The paper used in this publication meets the minimum requirements of the American National Standard for
Information Sciences—Permanence of Paper for Printed Library Materials, ANSI Z39.48-1992.

Do not now seek the answers, which cannot be given you because you would not be able to live them. And the point is, to live everything. Live the questions now. Perhaps you will then gradually, without noticing it, live along some distant day into the answer.

—RAINER MARIA RILKE

For Jack, Will, Sadie, Charlie, and Meghan. I love you more than George.

Contents

Introduction

It just may be that the most radical act we can commit is to stay home. What does that mean to finally commit to a place, to a people, to a community?

It doesn't mean it's easy, but it does mean you can live with patience, because you're not going to go away. It also means commitment to bear witness, and engaging in "casserole diplomacy" by sharing food among neighbors, by playing with the children and mending feuds and caring for the sick. These kinds of commitment are real. They are tangible. They are not esoteric or idealistic, but rooted in the bedrock existence of where we choose to maintain our lives.

That way we begin to know the predictability of a place. We anticipate a species long before we see them. We can chart the changes, because we have a memory of cycles and seasons; we gain a capacity for both pleasure and pain, and we find the strength within ourselves and each other to hold these lines.

That's my definition of family. And that's my definition of love.

—Terry Tempest Williams

I DIDN'T SET OUT to put down roots in a small town on Lake Superior, but thanks to a red sailboat and a sense of adventure, here I am, firmly planted in Bayfield. And like the best of epic tales, this one began with a journey on a boat, in our case with a bunch of kids and a 150-pound Newfoundland dog named Guinness. My husband, Ted, and our three children at the time, Jack, Will, and Sadie, sailed from Duluth, Minnesota, to Bayfield in June 2000 on our thirty-foot sailboat, *Isle of Skye*. Until then, my experience with Wisconsin didn't extend much beyond Polk County, where my parents have a raspberry farm, and thoughts of islands, ferries, and sea caves seemed fantastical. Given my seasickness issues, I slept the entire trip from Duluth to Bayfield, and I woke up just as we pulled into Justice Bay on Sand Island. I couldn't believe what I was seeing: brownstone cliffs, lighthouses, and crystal-clear blue water. I fell in love with the Apostle Islands as we sailed from Sand Island to Bayfield that June morning, and the deal was sealed when we pulled into the Bayfield harbor. I was home.

Our June visit, originally planned for a week, stretched into the fall and through our first Apple Fest, and by the following summer we had our own slip in the Apostle Islands Marina. Over the next six years we added two more children to our family, along with two more dogs, a trawler, and a house with a wraparound porch on Rittenhouse Avenue. Bayfield had become the place we dreamed of when we were at "home" in Minnesota, waiting for Friday, when we could head north again.

In 2007 we took the leap and moved to Bayfield full-time to open Good Thyme Restaurant and live our lives against the backdrop of waterfalls, beaches, and a quintessential small town of 487 people. I quickly learned that restaurant ownership doesn't mix well with five kids, four dogs, a ten o'clock bedtime, photography, reading, gardening, and cooking for my friends and family. In 2012 I sold my interest in the restaurant to my business partner and set out to rediscover my own kitchen table.

Here I am, many years later, with a whole lot of lessons learned, a much wider cooking repertoire (having limited takeout options means that if I want naan, Thai, or moo shu pork, I'd better get busy), and a greater appreciation for what it means to live in a northern Wisconsin town. Sure, I miss my favorite Greek grocery store, the Thai restaurant where we ordered by numbers, fresh tamales from West St. Paul, and oysters—I really miss oysters. But like so many immigrants before me, I adapted. I stock up on Greek olive oil and Thai fish sauce when I visit my family in Minneapolis. I make my own meatballs, pâté, pho, and ravioli. I haven't figured out the oyster situation yet, but I'm working on it (there's a beach party in my future featuring bivalves and champagne, I feel it in my bones). I've found ways to incorporate what grows and is raised in northern Wisconsin into my family's favorites, bringing together at our table what we carried with us into Bayfield and what we're learning about our new community. The name of the game in my kitchen is using local ingredients to cook globally and regionally inspired dishes. Fresh fruits and vegetables and local cheeses, eggs, meats, and grains are abundant on the Bayfield peninsula and in the Chequamegon Bay region. I've made pho with beef bones from a farm in Mellen, a soufflé with goat cheese made in Herbster, Indian chicken curry with curry powder from Washburn, and the best chowder with corn and potatoes from a farm stand in Ashland. Can I explain how a trip to Devil's Island in July makes me think of Cuban pork with a garlicky mojo sauce for dinner? Not in any way that makes logical sense, but it does.

Life's too short to let a little thing like mastering the art of sourdough bread, fresh pasta, or shoreline shrimp boils get in the way of a good meal. And it's too short to spend all my time in the kitchen. It's fantastically beautiful living on the shores of Lake Superior. The water is icy cold and crystal clear, white and

red pines poke their heads up over the forest canopy, and I can see every single star in the night sky. As I've knit myself into this community, I've learned that my experiences aren't unique. Generations of men and women have stood on these beaches, listened to water rushing over these basalt rocks, and picked wild blueberries here well before I sailed into the Bayfield harbor. The families of those men and women are still here, tethered to a place where they can slip behind their ancestor's eyes and take in essentially the same view. To focus solely on food would tell only part of the story of what and why I cook. My visits into the natural world, the stories of the families who've raised their children here, and my deep love and gratitude for Chequamegon Bay and the Apostle Islands are the invisible legs under my kitchen table, keeping me rooted to this place.

*　*　*

Food is my connection to the world. It's how I make friends, how I nourish my family, and how I define myself. But it wasn't until September 2014, when I learned about a proposed factory farm with twenty-six thousand Iowan hogs moving to Bayfield County, and when I also signed the contract for this book, that I fully grasped the intricate relationship between food and community. Buying locally or sustainably raised meats or vegetables isn't important because they taste better (although they do). It's important because all food comes with consequences, good or bad, for the community where it's grown.

Until I had to live with the prospect of those twenty-six thousand hogs living in the Lake Superior basin, for some reason my idea of local or sustainable didn't extend to meat. I've always tried to buy local produce, milk, and eggs, but when I needed a Boston butt or a ribeye steak, I purchased my plastic-wrapped piece of meat without once thinking about the people who lived near the factory farm that produced my dinner.

But as I considered the impact of a factory farm in our region—of millions of gallons of manure so near Lake Superior—I knew I had start making changes in my own kitchen. It boils down to this: all food comes from someplace—from some *place*—and the food grown or raised in Bayfield is possible because of our healthy soil and clean water. It took my love of Bayfield, my commitment to one of the last places on earth with abundant fresh and clean water, to fully develop my stance on local, sustainably grown or raised food. The old adage that "you are what you eat" should be expanded to "how what you eat is raised matters" because community and food are intertwined. And as with all complex questions, our answers will be as diverse as the food on our tables and the people sitting around them.

Creating change requires a series of meaningful decisions that support our values—from the food we eat to the places where we choose to spend our lives. And it requires small steps, steps that say, I don't have all the answers, but I know enough to ask the questions that will define what I hold dear. These first steps happen in our homes: we start where we stand and make the road by walking. Our personal approach to food doesn't have to be a precious manifesto. It just has to be authentic, to be real enough to admit that not every day is about homemade puff pastry or changing the world, but that there are moments of wonder, gratitude, and connection that live amidst and within us.

Gathering people around my table is a constant theme for me, as are the places, friends, dogs, food, and family who contribute to the cauldron of my food inspiration. I follow the breadcrumb trail of that inspiration to my local farm stands, beaches, or waterfalls—or into the unknown. Sometimes I end up in a stand of hemlocks in the middle of nowhere, and other times I end up with a pig's head boiling on the stove for head cheese. I never know where the inspiration will take me, and frankly, knowing would take the joy out of it for me. These recipes, photos, and stories are my way-markers on a spectacular journey. **Let's dig in!**

How To Use a Cookbook
Written at a Kitchen Table

THIS BOOK WAS WRITTEN AND PHOTOGRAPHED in a kitchen full of kids, dogs, backpacks, coffee cups, soccer cleats, opened wine bottles, and lots of papers: homework, permission slips, mail, and recipe notes. I'm a big believer that what happens in the kitchen is a strange brew of inspiration, intuition, and creativity, and up until I wrote this book, I rarely measured, used a timer, or followed a recipe. These recipes are guidelines, a place to start in *your* kitchen, and while I've made every recipe in this book many times, there's no guarantee that what you cook from this book will come out tasting exactly like it did in my kitchen.

I want to share the experience of cooking with you through these pages, and at times you may encounter gaps in our conversation. Think of them as opportunities to explore your own ideas, to trust your instincts, and to create your own version of what's in the book. Taste, look, poke, smell, and feel your way to the table; it's your meal, after all!

Spring

LAKE SUPERIOR is our bellwether for spring. In early March, we begin to look for the telltale signs of blue water among the ice sheets and the sounds of groaning and cracking, followed by the tinkling of candled ice, that tell us the lake is shedding its winter cloak. Then we watch for the first ferry to make its way to Madeline Island, cutting a path through the melting ice, a sure sign that winter doesn't last forever. Winter is a persistent beast up here and tends to toss a couple of rogue snowstorms our way in March and April that give me a chance to make one last pot of stew and pull out the mukluks for a final spin. However, what spring lacks in persistence in April it makes up for with productivity in May. Overnight, the grass greens up, bright shoots of future flowers poke through the soil in the garden, our fruit trees set buds, the hillsides start to change from brown to green, and ramps and mushrooms reveal themselves on the forest floor. It's almost shocking how quickly the earth wakes up and immediately gets down to the business of regeneration and growth. All that bright green newness inspires me to shake off the winter lethargy and begin planning our gardens and our summer adventures, setting the stage for the growth and harvest that are to come.

Northernmost
Sugarbush

I GREW UP IN MINNEAPOLIS, where experience with syrup involved a plastic bottle shaped like a kind, matronly lady named Mrs. Butterworth. We had "real" maple syrup at home, but the über sweet syrup from the missus was my favorite. While I knew maple syrup came from trees, I was a babe in the sugar maple woods when it came to the nuts and bolts of a syrup operation.

Fast-forward thirty-five years, and I'm on my way to Julie and Charly's sugarbush, armed with cheese and smoked sausages and ready for my first opportunity to be a sap-hauling cog in the syrup-making machine. Julie and Charly hold the enviable title of Wisconsin's northernmost sugarbush: their stand of sugar maples is tucked away near the tip of the Bayfield peninsula, surrounded by tribal land. They met the Newago brothers, members of the Red Cliff Band of Lake Superior Chippewa, more than ten years ago and learned how to haul buckets, tap trees, and boil sap from a family that has been making maple syrup for many generations.

I heard about George and Keith Newago from Charly, but it wasn't until I visited their sugarbush, about a twenty-minute hike through hemlock and maple trees, that I understood how Julie and Charly

Continued on next page

became entranced with turning sap into syrup. The Newagos have an entirely different setup from Julie and Charly's—from the smoke-stained kettle over an open fire to the cedar log cabin built by hand to the journal filled with entries about weather, putting up firewood, and visitors going back twenty years—but the end result is the same: dark amber syrup ladled into jars and bottles. Bitten by the maple syrup bug, when the property next to the Newagos' came up for sale, Julie and Charly jumped headfirst into their own maple syrup operation—Northwoods apprenticeship at its best. Their 219 syrup (the name is a reference to maple syrup's boiling point) is a medium amber color with a caramelized-sugar-meets-mildly-smoked-maple flavor with a wisp of vanilla. In other words, seriously good.

It was a warm day when we visited in early March. The sap was rolling in the evaporator, wood smoke perfumed the air, the kids built a series of bridges over the stream, George (my yellow Labrador) was running amok, and Julie and I rinsed out the sap buckets. The whole afternoon felt timeless. Don't get me wrong, making syrup is a tremendous amount of work—tapping the trees, hauling buckets (back and forth, back and forth), cutting firewood, tending the fire, watching the temperature of the syrup, and Lord knows what else goes into maintaining a sugarbush—but the heart of the process hasn't changed for hundreds of years. Tap trees, build a fire, and boil the sap into syrup.

The warmth combined with happy kids, dogs, and good friends was as intoxicating as the smell of sap transforming into syrup. Maybe that's why sugarbushes are so enchanting—they signal a time when the trees are waking up, the sun is a little higher on the horizon, and snow is giving way to the green and muddy earth. Maple syrup: capturing spring awakenings in a bottle, one year at a time.

Wild Rice Blueberry Buttermilk Pancakes

Wild rice, or manoomin, plays a major ceremonial, spiritual, and sustenance role in the lives of the Ojibwe people in my community. It is part of the Obijwe story of migration from the East Coast to Lake Superior—prophecies told them to "go to the place where food grows on water." They ultimately settled here on the shores of Lake Superior and along inland lakes in the northern portions of Michigan, Wisconsin, and Minnesota because of the abundance of wild rice. The Kakagon Sloughs, on the shores of Lake Superior and on the Bad River reservation, is one of the largest natural wild rice beds in the world and has been designated as a Wetland of International Importance.

Wild rice is technically not a rice but an aquatic grass, harvested by hand in late summer to early fall. It has a rich, nutty taste and chewy texture and is well-suited to sweet or savory dishes. I've been the lucky recipient of freshly hand-parched wild rice, and it's an entirely different food than the paddy-cultivated wild rice that graced my childhood table.

SERVES 6

1¼ cups all-purpose flour
1 tablespoon sugar
1 teaspoon baking powder
½ teaspoon baking soda
½ teaspoon kosher salt
2 eggs
1¼ cups buttermilk
3 tablespoons maple syrup, plus more for serving
2 tablespoons vegetable oil
1½ cups cooked wild rice (about ½ cup uncooked rice)
Butter, for cooking and serving
½–1 cup frozen blueberries, thawed and drained

Combine flour, sugar, baking powder, baking soda, and salt in a large bowl. In a separate bowl, whisk the eggs, buttermilk, maple syrup, and oil until thoroughly combined. Add to the dry ingredients, mix until just combined, and fold in the wild rice.

Heat a skillet or griddle over medium heat until hot. Melt a small pat of butter on the griddle and immediately ladle half-cup portions of batter onto pan. Add a sprinkling of blueberries to each pancake and cook until golden brown, 3 to 4 minutes, then flip and cook the other side. Repeat with remaining batter. Serve with maple syrup and butter.

Poached Duck Egg with Asparagus Bundles and Maple Bacon Vinaigrette

Dana and Kathy, good friends of ours in Bayfield, had a sassy and very spunky duck named Phyllis—a quacking force to be reckoned with. I'm pretty sure she has a touch of post-traumatic stress disorder, because a bobcat filled his belly with her duck companions last year, and the quacking is her way of letting that bobcat know she's still standing. She celebrates every day with a chorus of quack, quack, quacking, and now that she has three new duck pals to boss around, she's happy.

When Kathy came over for dinner and handed me a container full of duck eggs, I was so happy and thankful Phyllis outfoxed that bobcat. Duck eggs have the most lovely, rich yolk, and to me that means two things: poached eggs or hollandaise sauce. Since I had a quart of Julie and Charly's 219 maple syrup and a package of prosciutto in the fridge, I settled on a salad topped with a poached egg, and prosciutto-wrapped asparagus bundles with a maple bacon vinaigrette. I've always loved that old-school spinach salad with a hard-boiled egg and warm bacon dressing, and this version is an homage to that salty and egg-y salad.

SERVES 4

FOR THE SALAD DRESSING

5	strips bacon, chopped
5	tablespoons sherry vinegar
3	tablespoons real maple syrup
1	tablespoon honey
1	teaspoon minced shallot
¼	cup olive oil
1½	teaspoons Dijon mustard
	Salt and pepper to taste

FOR THE SALAD

¼	cup olive oil, divided
1	Vidalia onion, sliced
1	large bunch of asparagus, washed and trimmed
5–7	pieces of prosciutto (depending on how many bundles you end up with)
	Salt and pepper to taste
12	ounces spinach or lettuce, washed
4	duck eggs (can substitute chicken eggs)

Put bacon in a medium skillet and cook over medium heat. Cook until bacon is golden brown and remove pan from heat. Transfer bacon to a paper towel, reserving 4 tablespoons of drippings in the pan. Whisk vinegar, maple syrup, honey, and shallot into the drippings. Return the pan to medium heat, bring vinaigrette to a simmer, and cook until slightly thickened, 3 to 5 minutes. Whisk in olive oil and mustard until incorporated and then stir in bacon pieces. Season with salt and pepper to taste. Transfer dressing to a bowl and set aside.

Place 2 tablespoons of oil in a large sauté pan and add the sliced onions. Cook over medium heat until the onions are golden brown and caramelized, about 20 minutes. Remove from pan and keep warm.

Preheat oven to 400°F and line a sheet tray with parchment. Make a bundle of 3 to 5 asparagus spears and wrap with one piece of prosciutto. Place on sheet tray. Continue with remaining asparagus and prosciutto. Drizzle the remaining 2 tablespoons of olive oil over the bundles, sprinkle with salt and pepper, and place in oven. Bake until the prosciutto is crisp and the asparagus is softened, 15 to 20 minutes. Remove from the oven and set aside.

About 10 minutes after you put the asparagus in the oven, poach eggs for runny yolks, 6 to 8 minutes.

Divide the salad greens among four plates. Top with onions, asparagus bundles, and poached eggs. Spoon the warm bacon vinaigrette over the top and serve immediately.

Sugarbush Margarita

I have a fondness for tequila, specifically a double Patrón on the rocks with three limes. Charly understands my penchant for tequila, and the last time I was at his sugarbush he offered me a margarita. A margarita in the 'bush? Now that was a stroke of brilliance.

When the Pagan Dinner Club, our monthly dinner club celebrating food and wine, next convened at Dana and Kathy's, the talk turned to Charly's syrup. As we were coming up with new and exciting ways to use 219 syrup, I remembered that first sugarbush margarita. My version of a sugarbush margarita began to take shape in my head, and I knew what I'd be doing on Sunday—experimenting with my favorite liquor and my favorite syrup. As luck would have it, I had a jar of 219 syrup, a bunch of blood oranges, and fresh limes. After a few quaffable trials and errors, I hit upon the right proportions of sweet syrup, orange and lime juices, and good tequila. Here's to a spring full of warmish days, cold nights, free-flowing sap, and sugarbush margaritas.

MAKES 2 DRINKS

2 tablespoons maple sugar
2 tablespoons Tajin Clásico Seasoning
4 ounces reposado tequila (I used Espolon 100 percent agave tequila)
3 ounces freshly squeezed blood orange juice (you can substitute regular orange juice, but this truly is its most delicious made with blood orange juice!)
3 ounces freshly squeezed lime juice
2 ounces maple syrup
Ice

Mix the maple sugar and Tajin together and place in a shallow bowl. Dip the rims of 2 rocks glasses in lime juice and then dip into the maple sugar/Tajin mixture. Fill the glasses with ice and set aside.

Place the tequila, blood orange juice, lime juice, and maple syrup in a cocktail shaker filled with ice. Shake vigorously for about 15 seconds and then divide between the glasses and serve.

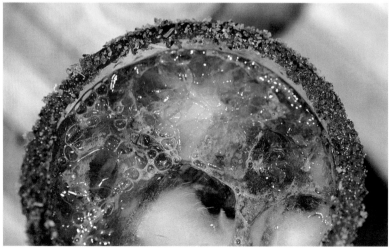

Maple Meringue Cookies

Maple sugar is one of the many gifts of spring. It's a good substitute for white sugar, and its subtle maple flavor is a great addition to quick breads and cookies. There is something infinitely satisfying about piping row after row of meringue cookies on the sheet tray, a reminder of the winter just passed: pillowy little snowdrifts infused with the flavor of spring.

MAKES ABOUT 4 DOZEN COOKIES

6   egg whites
¼   teaspoon cream of tartar
     Pinch of salt
1   cup maple sugar, plus more for
     sprinkling on top of cookies
½   cup raw sugar

Preheat the oven to 200°F. Line two sheet trays with parchment and set aside. Beat egg whites, cream of tartar, and pinch of salt until soft peaks form. Gradually add the maple and raw sugars and continue to beat until egg whites are shiny and hold stiff peaks.

Place the meringue in a pastry bag or a gallon-size plastic bag with the corner snipped off and pipe 1-inch cookies onto the sheet trays. Place in the oven and bake for 1 hour. Turn off the oven and let cool (with the oven door slightly ajar) for 45 minutes longer. Remove from oven and let cool. Store in an airtight container.

Maple Doughnuts

In our family, you're either a cook or a baker, and I am a cook; following directions is not my strong suit, and there isn't much room for improv when you're trying to make a cake. But my mom is a baker, and as luck and DNA would have it, my youngest daughter, Meghan, has become the baker in our house. Since we were in the midst of the springtime maple syrup season, she set out to find a doughnut worthy of freshly collected maple sap boiled into syrup. And she succeeded—these pillowy, maple-glazed doughnuts proved to be a fine homage to spring's maple sap run.

FOR THE DOUGHNUTS

¾	cup lukewarm milk
⅓	cup shortening
½	cup warm water
1½	tablespoons instant yeast (I use SAF red instant yeast)
⅓	cup maple sugar
1	teaspoon kosher salt
4½	cups all-purpose flour, divided
2	eggs
1	tablespoon vanilla
	Vegetable oil for greasing bowl and for frying

FOR THE MAPLE GLAZE

½	cup maple sugar
¼	cup butter
1	cup powdered sugar
¼	teaspoon cinnamon

In a small saucepan, heat the milk and shortening over medium-low heat until the shortening is melted; set aside to cool slightly. Combine the warm water and yeast in small bowl and set aside. Place the maple sugar and salt in the bowl of a stand mixer and then add the water/yeast and the milk/shortening mixtures. Using the paddle attachment, mix on medium speed until combined.

Add 1 cup of the flour, eggs, and vanilla and beat until smooth. Switch to the dough hook and add the remaining flour, ½ cup at a time, until the dough is pulling away from the sides of the bowl. Knead until the dough is smooth, about 1 minute. The dough will be slightly sticky. Place it in a large greased bowl, flip it around a few times to coat with the oil, cover loosely with plastic wrap, and let rise until doubled in size, about 30 to 45 minutes, in a warm place.

While the dough is rising, prepare the maple glaze. In a saucepan, melt the maple sugar and butter over medium heat until the sugar is completely dissolved. Whisk in the powdered sugar and cinnamon until smooth. Set aside until the doughnuts are fried and ready to be glazed.

When ready to roll out the dough, line a baking sheet with parchment paper. Lightly flour a work surface and roll out the dough to a ½-inch thickness. Using doughnut or cookie cutters, cut out 3-inch-diameter rounds with 1-inch-diameter holes. Arrange the doughnuts on the prepared baking sheet, leaving at least 1 inch between doughnuts. Cover the doughnuts with oiled plastic wrap and let them proof in a warm place until almost doubled in size, 45 to 60 minutes.

In a cast-iron pan or deep fryer, heat at least 2 inches of vegetable oil until a deep-fry thermometer registers 350°F. Working in batches, use a slotted metal spoon to carefully place the doughnuts in the hot oil. Fry doughnuts, flipping once, until light golden brown, 1 to 2 minutes per side. Transfer doughnuts to a wire rack and return the oil to 350°F between batches. Allow to cool for about 15 minutes and then glaze with maple glaze.

Spring Camp Falls

There are, it seems, two muses: the Muse of Inspiration, who gives us inarticulate visions and desires, and the Muse of Realization, who returns again and again to say, "It is yet more difficult than you thought." This is the muse of form. It may be then that form serves us best when it works as an obstruction, to baffle us and deflect our intended course. It may be that when we no longer know what to do, we have come to our real work and when we no longer know which way to go, we have begun our real journey. The mind that is not baffled is not employed. The impeded stream is the one that sings.

—Wendell Berry, *Standing by Words: Essays*

MY SON WILL AND I HAVE VISITED quite a few waterfalls in the past year, but Spring Camp Falls was one of the loveliest. We started the day headed toward Potato Falls, but after failing to get close enough to the falls and climbing up the steepest riverbank I've been on in thirty years (I'm terrified of heights), we decided to try to find Spring Camp Falls. I had seen a description of it online before we left, and the sum total of what I remembered was that it was outside of Hurley, somewhere. Since I knew how to get to Hurley and had a full tank of gas, at least four hours until dark, and a car full of adventurous people (and George, the yellow Lab), we decided to drive until we got cell service, Google the location, and take a few photos. If only it had been that easy.

Here are the directions (from the Travel Wisconsin site):

"Heading south from Hurley on US 51, travel about 4.5 mi to County Road C. Turn right (west). About 1.5 mi west, the county road will take a sharp turn north—don't take that. Continue forward on the gravel road. About 1 mi, turn to the south, following the."

Following the . . . what? As I drove down dirt roads to nowhere, Will and I tried to fill in the blank. Following the river, the yellow brick road, the pied piper, the big sign that says "Spring Camp Falls this way"? I hate asking for directions, but it was getting late and I wasn't going to let my bullheadedness get in the way of a waterfall photo safari. After a wrong turn into someone's deer camp, we took a right at an intersection with a bunch of signs on the corner. We drove and drove and drove until we finally encountered an old man walking down the road. I stopped the car and asked if he lived around here, to which he answered, "All my life, about eighty-five years"—at least I'd had enough luck to find a knowledgeable direction provider. We thanked the man and traveled back the way we had come—right back to the intersection with all the signs and the one we had missed, "Spring Camp Falls 1 mile ahead."

We had started the day with Potato Falls as our destination, and instead we spent a couple of hours in the car driving through remarkably beautiful country, laughing over George stories, bickering about Will's music choices, and breathing the same air in the same space for a while. As Wendell Berry said, "It may be that . . . when we no longer know which way to go, we have begun our real journey," and while a road trip to a waterfall is a small thing compared to finding my real work, I'm so glad we took the long way around.

Two themes that have played over and over in my life's reel are surrender and acceptance. And believe me, my rudimentary understanding of those two words has been hard-won. I don't like to ask for directions, and I don't ever want to surrender. Surrendering means straying from the script I've written in my head and allowing someone or something else to take the reins—not exactly my cup of tea (or, more accurately, my glass of dry Spanish red wine). The challenges, detours, or roadblocks I've encountered were there because I was ready for the next thing. The thing I hadn't even dreamed of yet.

Surrendering to what's next isn't easy, but it does mean that the moment when you think "I have no idea what the hell I'm doing" is the moment you are starting to do exactly what you should be doing. Obstacles are not deal breakers; they are a chance for recalibration and to keep your eyes peeled for the sign that will lead you to your next destination. Impeded streams make the most beautiful music, especially when you've just come up for air after a ride down the waterfall.

South of the Border Chicken Soup

Sometimes a sprinkling of spice in soups, relationships, or your music playlist can make all the difference. Don't get me wrong, I love those six to eight months in Bayfield when the ground is snow covered, muddy, or brown, but come March or April, visions of ancho chile peppers and garden-fresh tomatoes start to dance in my head. This soup is my version of adding a little of Shakira's "Hips Don't Lie" to the Bon Iver playlist of late winter and early spring. Plus it's the perfect dinner after spending the afternoon lost on the country roads of Bayfield looking for an epic waterfall adventure.

SERVES 6

8 bone-in chicken thighs
2 tablespoons olive oil
½ medium yellow onion, chopped
4 cloves garlic, minced
1 teaspoon cumin
1 teaspoon ancho chile powder
1 teaspoon kosher salt
½ teaspoon black pepper
6 cups chicken stock
2 medium sweet potatoes, peeled and cut into bite-sized pieces
1 can (28 ounces) chopped tomatoes, drained
1 cup corn kernels (fresh or frozen)
2 tablespoons freshly squeezed lime juice
¼ cup chopped fresh cilantro (stems and leaves), plus extra for serving
Avocado, sliced
Monterey Jack cheese, shredded
Tortilla chips, crumbled, for garnish

Preheat oven to 400°F. Place the chicken thighs on a parchment-lined sheet tray and cook until skin is crispy and the internal temperature reaches 165°F, about 30 minutes. Remove from oven and let cool. When cool enough to handle, remove and discard skin, shred meat, and set aside.

In a large stockpot over medium heat, heat the olive oil. Add the onions and sauté until softened, about 10 minutes. Then add the garlic, cumin, ancho chile powder, salt, and pepper. Cook, stirring frequently, until fragrant, about another minute.

Add the chicken stock and sweet potatoes. Bring to a boil and then reduce heat to medium-low, cover, and simmer until sweet potatoes are tender, about 10 minutes. Add the shredded chicken, tomatoes, corn, lime juice, and cilantro and simmer until heated through, about 5 minutes. Serve with avocado, cheese, cilantro, and tortilla chips.

Spicy Cauliflower and Potato Soup

SERVES 6

1   head cauliflower, cored and cut into florets
4   cups peeled and cubed red potatoes
2   tablespoons olive oil
2½ teaspoons kosher salt, divided
1½ teaspoons black pepper, divided
1   tablespoon butter
½   cup chopped sweet onion
4   celery stalks, sliced ¼ inch thick
1   tablespoon minced garlic
4   cups chicken stock (preferably homemade or low sodium)
½   cup milk
½   cup cream
1   cup shredded Monterey Jack cheese
1   cup shredded Swiss cheese
½   cup Frank's Red Hot sauce (can use less if you are heat averse)

Preheat oven to 400°F. Line a sheet tray with parchment and set aside. Toss the cauliflower and potatoes in a large bowl with the olive oil, 1 teaspoon salt, and ½ teaspoon pepper. Roast until tender, about 30 minutes.

While the cauliflower and potatoes are in the oven, heat the butter in a large Dutch oven or heavy-bottomed stockpot and sauté the onions and celery with the remaining salt and pepper until softened, about 10 minutes. Add the garlic and cook until fragrant. Set aside until the cauliflower and potatoes are out of the oven.

Add the chicken stock, roasted cauliflower, and potatoes to the Dutch oven and bring to a boil. Simmer 30 minutes, uncovered. Using an immersion blender, puree the soup and then add the milk and cream. Add the cheeses and hot sauce and stir until the cheese is melted, Serve immediately.

Curried Carrot Soup

Back in the days of sippy cups and Disney backpacks, carrots were a vehicle for buttermilk ranch dressing. I never would have guessed my kids would eat, let alone request, curried carrot soup. But just like I never imagined being the shortest person in the family or handing them the car keys, it happened, and it's been a pleasant surprise. Carrots are a staple in my northern kitchen; they are available all year long and are as versatile as those other stalwart root vegetables, potatoes, squash, and rutabagas, that grace our dinner table. This soup is light and brightly flavored. Think of it as a harbinger of the summer days to come.

SERVES 6

- 2 tablespoons coconut oil
- 1 sweet onion, chopped
- 1 teaspoon kosher salt, plus more to taste
- ½ teaspoon cracked pepper, plus more to taste
- 2 cloves garlic, minced
- 2 tablespoons minced ginger
- 2 tablespoons curry powder
- 4 cups chicken stock (preferably homemade or low sodium)
- 2 cans (13.5 ounces each) coconut milk
- 6 cups peeled and rough-chopped carrots (about 8 carrots)
- ¼ cup rough-chopped fresh cilantro
- 1 tablespoon lime juice

Heat the coconut oil in a heavy-bottomed stockpot or Dutch oven and add the onion, salt, and pepper and cook over medium heat for 10 minutes. Add the garlic, ginger, and curry powder and cook until fragrant, about another minute. Add the chicken stock, coconut milk, and carrots and bring to a boil. Reduce heat to medium-low, cover, and simmer until carrots are soft, 15 to 20 minutes. Add the cilantro and lime juice and stir to combine.

Using an immersion blender, puree the soup until smooth. Season with salt and pepper and serve immediately.

Sara Ann's Kazingas

Every young girl needs a Sara Ann in her life: a woman who will introduce her to the importance of a good book, a naughty dog, a properly cooked prime rib, an unflagging devotion to those you love, and the sense of freedom (and frustration) that only a convertible MG can provide. Sara Ann, my mother's cousin and my de facto godmother, was a constant presence during my childhood—at every birthday party, Christmas Eve dinner, and Easter brunch—and these zingy little cheese crackers were her signature contribution to the cocktail hour. They are the grown-up version of Cheez-Its, incredibly easy to pull together, and the perfect accompaniment to a hearty bowl of soup or a Bombay gin martini.

MAKES ABOUT 6 DOZEN CRACKERS

- ½ cup cold butter, cut into small pieces
- ½ pound shredded cheddar cheese (about 2 cups)
- 1¼ cups all-purpose flour
- ½ teaspoon kosher salt
- ¼ teaspoon cayenne
- 4 tablespoons water, plus more if needed

Place all ingredients except water in the bowl of a food processor and pulse until the mixture resembles coarse sand. Add the water, a teaspoon at a time, until the dough starts to come together into a ball.

Turn the dough out onto a large piece of wax or parchment paper. Roll the dough into a log 9 or 10 inches long. Wrap well and refrigerate until firm, 2 hours or longer. (You can freeze the dough for up to 1 month).

Preheat oven to 375°F and line a sheet tray with parchment paper. Cut the log into ¼-inch-thick slices. Arrange the slices about 1 inch apart on the sheet tray. Bake until the crackers are a light golden color, 8 to 10 minutes. Turn the crackers and bake until they are golden around the edges, 3 to 5 more minutes. Transfer to a wire rack and let cool. Store in an airtight container at room temperature for up to 5 days.

Asparagus with Anchovy Butter

We're lucky that wild asparagus grows on the hillside next to our house, and if I can get to it before the dogs, it's one of our first fresh-from-the-ground vegetables in the spring. While fresh asparagus needs little more than butter, salt, and pepper to shine, I was looking for a preparation with a little more oomph. Alongside the forty-five types of mustards, pickles, and Thai fish sauce in the fridge, there's always a little jar of anchovies in olive oil—they're my secret ingredient in stews, salad dressings, and sauces. Anchovies and asparagus; who knew? They are a match made in little fishy heaven, and the combination takes plain old asparagus to a new level of fancy-schmancy.

SERVES 4

- 1 bunch fresh asparagus, washed and ends trimmed
- ¾ cup dry white wine
- 2 tablespoons minced shallots
- 2 tablespoons chopped fresh Italian parsley
- 1 garlic clove, minced
- ¼ cup butter
- 4 anchovies in olive oil, chopped
- 1 tablespoon capers
- Maldon sea salt and pepper
- ¼ cup grated Parmesan cheese
- 2 tablespoons pine nuts, toasted

Trim asparagus stalks to the same length. Bring a large pot of salted water to a boil, add asparagus, and boil until cooked but still crisp, 3 to 4 minutes. Drain on a towel.

In a medium saucepan, combine wine, shallots, parsley, and garlic and simmer until the wine is reduced by half. Add the butter and whisk until it is melted. Add the anchovies and capers and stir to combine. Taste for seasoning and add salt and pepper if necessary. Place the asparagus on a platter, pour the butter sauce over it, and garnish with Parmesan and pine nuts. Serve immediately.

Sassy Nanny Birthing Day

"TWO GOATS WORKING ON IT. Come when you can if you want to witness a birth!" It's not every day you get a text like that, and I wasn't about to miss my chance to experience the miracle of birth as a spectator, not an active participant. I had eaten pounds of my friend Michael's Sassy Nanny goat cheese and had even taken pictures at his farm, but I'd never attended the birth of baby goats (or baby anything else, for that matter). I grabbed a bottle of champagne, some tom kha gai soup for lunch, and bones for Zuzu and Rex (the resident goat-yard dogs), jumped in the car, and went off to my very first goat midwifery experience.

You'd think a woman who has delivered five ten-pound babies would be an old hand at the birth game, but it's not true. I took one look at the two girls, Lena and Donatella, getting ready to usher their little ones into the world and felt like Prissy in *Gone with the Wind*. Thank God Michael knows a whole lot about birthing babies, and he delivered each one with a sense of hard-won, calm competence. Watching the babies enter this world and come to life in front of my eyes filled me with a sense of wonder I haven't felt since I met my own babies for the first time.

As we were waiting for Donatella's second boy to arrive, her first decided to stretch his legs and stand up. Michael said he was one of the biggest baby goats he'd seen. The little guy was only about forty-five minutes old when he took his first unsteady steps toward Mama—a Herculean feat and so incredibly tender at the same time.

Lena's last baby, a girl, entered the world with a nearly showstopping maneuver; she had her head tucked under her back leg, which caused a great deal of chaos. Michael tried to grab ahold of her legs, but she was good and stuck. I started to get a little panicked but he kept his cool, methodically working to free her head. It was probably no more than three or four minutes, but time seemed to stand still while Michael got her straightened out, and we all breathed a sigh of relief when the little miss lifted her head and looked around.

I walked outside to gather myself after the last baby was born. It was an intense afternoon for a woman who up to this point had a) fainted at the sight of blood and b) hated the smell of amniotic fluid—making me not the most logical choice for a birthing day companion. I stood outside in the sunlight and looked around at all the life Michael has ushered into the world. Living your dream takes a tremendous amount of hard work—the stakes are high, and success is hard to measure. Michael, like most of my friends up here, chose the road less traveled. It makes a difference to live the life you've dreamed of, to be a good steward to your environment and animals, to live in the moment (especially when the moment is one you would rather fast-forward) with the courage to watch it all unfold and know it is as it should be. A little sass doesn't hurt either.

Herb-Marinated Goat Cheese

What's easier than bathing goat cheese in olive oil and herbs? Pulling it out of the refrigerator three days later, spooning it into a bowl, and serving it with slices of a crusty baguette. Think of it as the little black dress of appetizers: always appropriate and never overdone.

SERVES 8 AS AN APPETIZER WITH CRACKERS OR A SLICED BAGUETTE

½ teaspoon chopped fresh thyme
½ teaspoon chopped fresh oregano
¼ teaspoon chopped rosemary
1 clove garlic, minced
¼ teaspoon lemon zest
  Coarse cracked pepper to taste
8 ounces goat cheese
2 cups olive oil, or enough to cover
  the cheese
  Crackers or toasted baguette slices,
  for serving

In a small bowl, combine the herbs, garlic, lemon zest, and cracked pepper and mix until thoroughly combined. In a jar or bowl large enough to hold the goat cheese, layer the goat cheese with the herb mixture, making about 3 layers, and then pour enough olive oil over the layers to completely cover the cheese.

Cover the container with a lid or plastic wrap and store in the refrigerator to marinate for at least 24 hours and up to 5 days. Remove the cheese from the oil with a spoon, making sure to get some herbs and oil with the cheese (you can strain and reserve the rest of the oil for cooking or salad dressing). Serve with crackers or toasted baguette slices.

Herbed Goat Cheese Ravioli

Once I got the hang of making my own pasta, there was no looking back—plus I absolutely love working with the dough. There is something magical about the transformation from shaggy, floury mess to a pliant, silky dough. An herb and goat cheese combination isn't revelatory, but sometimes an old tried-and-true option is a good idea, and these are really, really good.

MAKES ABOUT 30 RAVIOLI

FOR THE FILLING

- 8 ounces goat cheese (I use Sassy Nanny Lake Effect)
- 5 ounces Sartori Balsamic Bellavitano cheese, shredded (can substitute Parmesan-Reggiano cheese)
- ½ cup whole-milk ricotta cheese
- 1 clove garlic, minced
- 2 teaspoons minced fresh thyme
- 2 teaspoons chopped fresh basil
- ¼ teaspoon red pepper flakes
  Salt and pepper to taste

FOR THE DOUGH

- 4 cups 00 (extra fine) flour, plus more for rolling out (can substitute all-purpose flour)
- 4 large eggs
- 3 tablespoons olive oil
- 1 teaspoon kosher salt
- ½ cup water, divided
- ¼ cup semolina flour or cornmeal, for dusting the sheet tray

Mix all the filling ingredients together in a large bowl and set aside while you make the pasta dough.

Place flour, eggs, olive oil, and salt in the bowl of a stand mixer. Turn the mixer on low and slowly add 3 tablespoons of the water. Add more water, 1 tablespoon at a time, until the mixture comes together and forms a ball. Knead the dough on a lightly floured board to make sure it is well mixed. Cover the dough with a bowl and let rest for 30 minutes.

Generously flour your work area. Cut the dough into 6 equal pieces and cover with a towel or a large bowl to keep it from drying out when you are rolling out the pasta sheets. With your hands, flatten and shape one piece of dough into a ½-inch-thick rectangle. Dust it lightly with flour and pass it through the widest setting on the pasta machine. If the dough comes out oddly shaped, reform into a rectangle. Fold it in thirds, like a letter, and if necessary, flatten to ½ inch thick. Pass it through the widest setting again with the seam of the letter perpendicular to the rollers. Repeat this folding and rolling step five or six times, dusting the dough with flour if it becomes sticky. This is an important step in pasta making: you want to work the dough until it becomes silky and elastic.

Without folding the dough, pass it through the next narrowest setting on the pasta machine. Keep reducing the space between the rollers after each pass, lightly dusting the pasta with flour on both sides each time (I stop at setting number 7 on the KitchenAid pasta roller).

Dust a sheet tray with semolina flour or cornmeal and set aside. Have about a cup of water and a pastry brush nearby when you are ready to form the ravioli. Dust the work surface and sheet of dough with flour. Lay out the long sheet of pasta and brush the top surface with water. Drop tablespoon-sized scoops of filling on the top half of the pasta sheet, about 2 inches apart. Brush the area between each mound of filling with water. Fold the other half of the dough over the filling like a blanket. Using your fingers, gently press out air pockets around each mound of filling. Use a sharp knife to cut each pillow into squares and crimp the 3 edges with a fork to make a tight seal, or use a ravioli cutter. Place the ravioli on the prepared sheet tray and set aside to dry slightly while you assemble the remaining ravioli.

Cook the ravioli in plenty of boiling salted water until they float to the top, 5 to 7 minutes (depending on how big they are). Carefully lift the ravioli from the water with a large strainer or slotted spoon. Serve immediately with your favorite tomato sauce and freshly grated Parmesan.

Sassy Salmon en Croute

There are a few things I always have in the freezer: meatballs, Tetzner's ice cream from Washburn, chicken stock, and puff pastry dough. That last item is my idea of a secret weapon—wrap just about anything in a buttery, flaky dough, and voilà, you've elevated the ordinary to the extraordinary (the power of butter is endless). Add a few dollops of Sassy Nanny goat cheese into the mix and you are situated for dinner success.

The last time I made this I tried to roll out the dough when it was too cold. It kept cracking, and I wasn't able to get it large enough to wrap up the entire fish. I decided to morph my "en croute" to "en galette" and wrapped the salmon about halfway up. It turned out to be a lucky detour—the filling (now the topping) ended up caramelized, and the puff stayed crisp because the moisture from the spinach and mushrooms evaporated in the oven. I guess impatience can pay off (sometimes).

SERVES 6

¼ cup butter
8 ounces fresh mushrooms, sliced
3 large shallots, chopped
2 packages (10 ounces each) frozen spinach, thawed and squeezed dry
2 cloves garlic, minced
½ cup sun-dried tomatoes in olive oil, chopped
2 tablespoons chopped fresh thyme
Salt and freshly ground black pepper to taste
1 sheet frozen puff pastry, thawed (half of a 17.3 ounce package; I use Pepperidge Farms)
1 salmon fillet (2 to 2½ pounds), skinned
1 large egg
2 teaspoons water
8 ounces goat cheese, divided into 8 pieces (I use Sassy Nanny Lake Effect)

Melt the butter over medium-high heat in a large skillet. Add the mushrooms and shallots and sauté until well cooked and all the liquid has evaporated, about 10 minutes. Add the spinach, garlic, sun-dried tomatoes, and thyme and sauté until all liquid is evaporated, about another 5 minutes. Season to taste with salt and pepper. Transfer to a covered container and refrigerate until thoroughly cooled, up to one day in advance.

Line a sheet tray with parchment paper. Lightly flour a clean work surface and set out the chilled puff pastry. Let the pastry sit just long enough to become pliable, so it won't break or crack when you unfold it and try to roll it out. Roll out the puff pastry dough to fit your salmon fillet when it's placed on the dough on the diagonal. Place the dough on the prepared sheet tray. In a small bowl, combine the egg and water for the egg wash and beat with a fork until foamy.

Season the salmon fillet with salt and pepper. Spread the spinach/mushroom/tomato mixture on top of the salmon fillet. Place the chunks of goat cheese evenly along the length of the salmon.

Wrap the dough up around the salmon (the dough will not cover the salmon entirely; there will be about 2 inches of the salmon and filling exposed). Brush the sides of the dough with the egg wash, being careful not to let too much egg drip down the edges of the pastry, and cover loosely with plastic wrap. Place in the refrigerator and chill for 1 hour before baking.

Preheat the oven to 450°F. Remove the plastic wrap, place the baking sheet on the center rack of the oven, and bake for 15 minutes. Decrease the temperature to 350°F and bake until the pastry is golden brown and puffed, 15 to 20 minutes longer. Remove from the oven and let rest, uncovered, for 10 minutes before cutting.

Olympia
Sport Village

I HAD NO IDEA THAT ATHLETES SHOT RIFLES in the Olympics until I had an opportunity to spend time at a resort near Hurley that trained Olympic athletes in the art of the biathlon (a 12.5-mile cross-country ski race combined with marksmanship) in the 1960s and 1970s. Bobbi and Tom, friends and fellow water lovers, hosted a Summit for the Bad River Watershed at Olympia Sport Village one spring, and as I plugged the address into my phone, I knew I was in for an adventure. From the looks of my Google map (before I lost my cell phone signal), I was going to be spending the night in the middle of nowhere.

Between the afternoon session and happy hour around the campfire, I wandered through the resort. The log cabins and main lodge are perched on a hill overlooking a spring-fed lake ringed by pines and maples. It's about as idyllic Northwoods Wisconsin as it gets: Adirondack chairs, a Leinenkugel beer sign, a stone fireplace, and cross-country skis hanging on the wall. The lodge was built as an executive retreat by one of the mining companies operating in the Ironwood area in the 1940s. The cabins and camp were erected in 1966 by Dr. Tom Rosandich, founder and president of the United States Sports Academy, as a facility to train physical education teachers and coaches for a variety of sports: track, cross-country, football, wrestling, and skiing. Rosandich spent a lot of time overseas prior to building the resort, and the inspiration for the facility came while he was working for the US State Department coaching track and field in Indonesia. His wife, Sally, was from the Hurley area, and they raised their six kids while running a nationally recognized year-round sports camp for young athletes and coaches.

But it was the biathlon that put Olympia on the map. In 1967 Olympia Sport Village hosted the National Biathlon Championship and the biathlon trials for the 1968 Winter Olympic Games in Grenoble, France. Wisconsin governor Warren Knowles even visited the camp and officially opened the championship and tryouts.

It was a one-of-a-kind camp in the 1960s, and it's a one-of-a-kind private residence now. I can't wait to visit it again. It's a time capsule of what makes northern Wisconsin special: remnants of the culture of summers spent at the lake, drinks served in a bar with wood-paneled walls, and cabins infused with the smells of wet bathing suits and campfires. And that's a rare bird these days.

Preserved Lemons

Citrus is a bright spot in my kitchen during the winter and spring seasons. While I love root vegetables as much as the next gal, you can't zest a potato to add zip to Thai curry or squeeze some juice from a turnip for a salad dressing. Sometimes I want more complexity than a tablespoon of zest or juice can provide, and that's where preserved lemons come in. They bring a punch of salty, lemony flavor to a roast chicken, a salad dressing, or a Moroccan cheeseball, and I find myself reaching for them whenever a dish needs a little "something." Their bright citrus flavor is a reminder that even in March, sunny days are happening somewhere in this country, and we northerners can squeeze, zest, or peel our way toward that warmth.

MAKES 1 JAR OF PRESERVED LEMONS

10–12 organic lemons, preferably Meyer lemons
½–1 cup kosher salt
Freshly squeezed lemon juice, if needed
1 cinnamon stick (optional)
2 dried Thai peppers (optional)

Using warm water, scrub each lemon and dry completely. Place about 1 tablespoon of kosher salt into an empty 1-quart mason jar. Quarter each lemon, slicing them down just over three-quarters of the way (do NOT cut all the way through; the slices need to be attached at the end) and then reshape the fruit into halves

Place about 1 teaspoon of kosher salt into each quartered lemon half, place lemon half (cut-side down) in the mason jar, press down firmly to release the juice, and put another teaspoon of salt on top of the lemon. Repeat this process with the remaining lemons, packing them as tightly as possible into the jar. Add the cinnamon stick and Thai peppers to the jar if you are using them. When the jar is full, the juice should cover the lemons; if it doesn't, add some additional fresh lemon juice.

Seal the jar and set aside, at room temperature, for 3 to 4 weeks. Shake the jar every day to keep the salt well distributed and store in the refrigerator once opened. Rinse the lemons before using.

Grapefruit and Juniper Gravlax

Salmon cured in salt, sugar, citrus zest, and spices: an homage to the practicality of curing and the beauty of the citrus harvest, all wrapped up in a salty/sweet package. Maybe it was the name, gravlax, or the idea of safely eating raw fish, but I assumed making gravlax was best left to the professionals and my job was to make a tangy sauce and slice the rye bread. I couldn't have been more wrong. Making gravlax is ridiculously easy and rewarding.

SERVES 12 TO 14 AS AN APPETIZER

½ cup kosher salt
⅓ cup raw sugar
Zest of 1 lemon
Zest of 1 grapefruit
2 tablespoons black peppercorns, cracked
1½ tablespoons chopped fresh ginger
1 tablespoon juniper berries, crushed
1 large shallot, thinly sliced
1 pound salmon fillet (about 1½ pounds), skin-on
1 medium bunch of fennel fronds, coarsely chopped
3 tablespoons chopped fresh dill
3 tablespoons salt-cured capers, rinsed and coarsely chopped
Rye bread, for serving

Place salt, sugar, lemon zest, grapefruit zest, peppercorns, ginger, juniper berries, and shallot in a bowl and mix to thoroughly combine. Cut a piece of plastic wrap twice as long as the salmon fillet and place it, unfolded, on a flat surface. Sprinkle about ⅓ of the salt mixture and ⅓ of the fennel fronds on the plastic wrap and lay the salmon, skin side down, on top of salt/fennel mixture. Sprinkle the remainder of the salt and chopped fennel on top of the fillet and tightly wrap the salmon in the plastic wrap (you may need additional pieces of plastic wrap). Carefully pierce the plastic wrap (taking care to not pierce the skin) and place on a wire rack set over a sheet tray (skin side down). Place another sheet tray on top of the salmon and weigh it down with large cans of tomatoes/beans/whatever you have in your cupboard. Refrigerate, turning once a day, until the salmon is firm, 2 to 3 days.

Rinse the excess salt mixture off the salmon under cold water, pat it dry, and thinly slice. Garnish with dill and capers and serve on sliced rye bread. The cured salmon will keep, tightly wrapped, in the refrigerator for about two weeks.

Moroccan Grapefruit Salad

I came across a Sicilian salad in David Tanis's cookbook *Heart of the Artichoke* with oranges, fennel, spinach, and radishes and thought it sounded like the perfect spring dish. I decided to introduce Sicily to Morocco and added some oil-cured olives and cilantro. The fennel went in the oven to be roasted, and I whipped up a vinaigrette. I am a firm believer in bright, acidic vinaigrettes, so I used raspberry and white wine vinegar as well as a healthy dollop of Dijon mustard. Dinner was looking better and better—until I opened the fridge to look for the orange, the shining star of my salad. I had grapefruits galore but not one orange. Grapefruit is round, grows on trees in Florida, and is kind of orange-colored—a perfectly suitable substitute, right? The pink grapefruit was beautiful against the green spinach, and its acidity was well suited for the dressing and olives.

SERVES 4

FOR THE SALAD

- A couple handfuls of baby spinach
- 2 grapefruits, peeled, quartered, and sliced
- 1 red onion, sliced and placed in ice water for 10 to 15 minutes (this removes the acidity from the onion)
- ¼ cup pitted and chopped oil-cured olives
- ¼ cup chopped fresh cilantro
- Maldon sea salt to taste

FOR THE VINAIGRETTE

- ½ cup good olive oil
- 2 tablespoons raspberry vinegar
- 2 tablespoons white wine vinegar
- 2 tablespoons Dijon mustard
- 2 tablespoons honey
- Salt and pepper to taste

Assemble the spinach, grapefruit, red onion, olives, and cilantro in a bowl. Salt to taste. Combine all vinaigrette ingredients in a container and pour over the salad.

Angel Pie

I'm not much of a dessert fan, but if it involves meringue or lemon curd, I'm all in. My Grandma Duffy was a big fan of this dessert, and I still remember the first time I tasted the rich and tangy creaminess of the lemon curd combined with the airiness of the meringue crust. I was hooked. Meringue and lemon curd are like Laverne and Shirley or Laurel and Hardy: where one leaves off, the other comes in. Meringue uses only the egg whites, and lemon curd uses the yolks . . . now, if that isn't a match made in heaven, I don't know what is.

MAKES 1 PIE

FOR THE MERINGUE SHELL

4	egg whites
¼	teaspoon cream of tartar
1	cup sugar

FOR THE LEMON CURD

4	egg yolks
½	cup sugar
⅓	cup freshly squeezed lemon juice
2	tablespoons lemon zest
6	tablespoons butter, cut into 6 pieces
1	tablespoon vanilla

FOR THE WHIPPED CREAM

1	cup whipping cream
2	tablespoons sugar

Preheat oven to 275°F and butter a deep-dish pie plate. Beat egg whites and cream of tartar until soft peaks form. Gradually add sugar. Continue to beat until egg whites are shiny and hold stiff peaks. Spread into pie plate. Bake for 20 minutes and then raise the oven temperature to 300°F and bake 40 minutes longer. Remove from oven and let cool.

While the meringue is cooling, beat the egg yolks until thick and lemon colored, then beat in the sugar gradually. Blend in the lemon juice and zest and place in the top of a double boiler. Add the butter and vanilla and cook over medium-high heat, whisking constantly, until thick. Remove the lemon curd from the double boiler and set aside to cool.

Whip the cream on high speed until soft peaks form. Add the sugar and beat until stiff peaks form. Spread half of the whipped cream on the meringue, and then spread the lemon curd. Spread the remaining whipped cream over the lemon curd, cover, and place in the refrigerator for at least 8 hours. Will keep in the refrigerator up to 24 hours.

Grandma Rose's Gnocchi

I LOVE TEACHING COOKING CLASSES, but it's nice to be the student every so often. And it's especially nice to be a student when your friend Gina is teaching you how to make pillowy little bundles of potato heaven. Before this, gnocchi was a meal I ordered at a restaurant, not a meal I would have attempted at home. The line between pillowy potato packages and watery potato soup seemed nebulous, and when I have a kitchen full of hungry kids, it's not wise to mess up the main dish. I needed an Italian to teach me the art of gnocchi, and Gina was the perfect instructor. And since my kitchen is built for a crowd, we invited ten friends and called it a party/cooking class.

Gina, like all good Italian women, came armed with an apron, her Grandma Rose's recipe, the tablecloth that she's been rolling gnocchi and pasta on for years, and a basket full of cooked and cooled russet potatoes. We sat around the table and shared stories of our favorite meals, memories of our grandmothers, and the nuances of rolling gnocchi (which is a lot harder than it looks). As I looked around the table, a feeling of thankfulness settled over me. Thankful for Gina and her stories of Grandma Rose, for Grandma Rose for teaching Gina the art of gnocchi, and for the women who helped bring our dinner to life.

Potato Gnocchi

SERVES 4 TO 6

- 2 pounds russet potatoes
- 1 cup all-purpose flour, divided, plus more for rolling out
- 2 egg yolks, lightly beaten
- 1 teaspoon kosher salt
  Your favorite sauce, for serving (sage and brown butter sauce is especially delicious!)

Preheat the oven to 400°F and heavily flour a work surface. Prick the potatoes all over with a fork and place them directly on the oven racks. Bake until tender, about 1 hour (depending on the size of the potatoes). Remove from the oven and immediately cut them lengthwise to release their steam.

It is very important to rice the potatoes while they are still hot in order to get as much steam/moisture out of the potato as possible; this will ensure you have a light and fluffy gnocchi. As soon as the potatoes are cool enough to handle (after about 5 minutes), scoop the flesh out of the skins, discard the skins, and run the flesh through a food mill/ricer over a wooden board or paper towel–lined sheet tray, creating an evenly shallow layer of potato. Using a fork, lightly toss the potatoes every 3 or 4 minutes until there is no steam escaping and they are cool to the touch but not cold.

Place the riced potatoes on floured work surface. Add the egg yolks, ⅔ cup of flour, and salt to the riced potatoes, and, using a bench scraper or a wooden spatula, incorporate the flour into the potatoes, scraping from the bottom of the pile and bringing it to the top, repeating until the flour and egg yolks are completely incorporated and adding additional flour if the dough is too sticky. Do not overwork the dough; you want to stop right when it becomes workable and holds together.

Line a sheet tray with parchment and sprinkle with flour. Divide the dough into four pieces and cover with a clean dish towel. Lightly dust a wooden board or pastry cloth with flour, and, working with one piece of dough at a time, roll each piece quickly and lightly into a long rope about ¾-inch in diameter. Using a sharp knife or bench scraper, cut dough rope into ¾-inch pieces, place on the sheet tray, and sprinkle with flour. Repeat with the remaining dough and let sit at room temperature, uncovered, for up to 1 hour.

After the gnocchi have rested, bring a large pot of salted water to boil. Place the gnocchi in the boiling water and cook just until they float to the top, 2 to 4 minutes. Drain, top with your favorite sauce, and serve immediately.

Pickled Ramps

Wild onions, ramps, *allium tricoccum*, wood leek: different words for the same pungent and fragrant spring gift from the forest floor. Ramps are prolific in the Bayfield area, and they are one of the first foods I harvest in the spring. My friend Ellen introduced me to the art of harvesting ramps, and for the first couple of harvests, I went a little nuts. Ramps made an appearance at nearly every meal for weeks until Ted looked at me and asked for a ramp hiatus. I had to agree, it was time to take a break, but I still had two or three pounds of the lovely wild onions in the fridge, and I was not about to waste them.

I decided pickling was the perfect way to preserve my foraged wild onions. As I stood at the sink, trimming and washing the last of those oniony bad boys, my mind wandered back to the day when I went out with Ted, the kids, and George the yellow Lab to harvest ramps near a rushing creek outside of Bayfield. Charlie scouted out the best ramp patches, Will wandered around with his camera, Sadie was trying to embrace the gnats swarming around her head, Meg and Ted were exploring, and George amazed us with his ability to scamper across a fallen tree over the creek. I bottled up that warm spring day with my family in each jar of wild onions I sealed. Food is love, plain and simple.

2 pounds ramps, cleaned, green leaves and roots removed (I leave some of the smaller leaves on)

8–10 springs of thyme (depending on how many jars you are using)

1 cup white wine vinegar

1 cup sugar

1 cup water

2 tablespoons chopped fresh ginger

1 tablespoon kosher salt

1½ teaspoons mixed peppercorns

1 teaspoon mustard seeds

½ teaspoon red pepper flakes

½ teaspoon fennel seeds

1 bay leaf

Prepare jars and lids: Place two 1-pint jars on rack in a large pot, add enough water to cover the jars, and bring to boil over high heat. Boil for 10 minutes, then turn off heat and allow jars to rest in the hot water. Meanwhile, put bands and lids in small saucepan and cover with water. Heat over medium heat until the water is simmering, then remove pan from heat and allow bands and lids to rest in hot water until ready to use.

Bring a large pan of salted water to a boil over high heat. Add ramps and cook until tender-crisp, about 45 seconds. Remove the onions from the boiling water and immediately place in an ice bath. Drain. Divide the ramps and sprigs of thyme between your sterilized canning jars.

Combine the remaining ingredients in a large saucepan and bring to a boil. Cook, stirring, until the sugar is dissolved, and then pour the mixture over the wild onions and seal jars. Let cool to room temperature and refrigerate for 2 to 3 weeks.

Note: Home canning carries food safety risks. For complete canning instructions, consult the University of Wisconsin Extension's many publications on home canning and preserving (http://fyi.uwex.edu/safepreserving) or the National Center for Home Food Preservation's resources (http://nchfp.uga.edu).

Wild Ramp Pesto

It took me a couple of attempts to get this pesto right—straight ramp pesto is a formidable beast. I don't think I've ever eaten something that strong before (my breath could have melted steel or at least repelled every mosquito in Bayfield County). I knew I needed to temper the beast while maintaining the distinctive wild onion–garlic flavor of a ramp fresh from the forest floor. I settled on spinach, basil, and sun-dried tomatoes, and they were exactly the companions those wild ramps needed to become a bit more civilized.

MAKES ABOUT 2 CUPS

10–12 ramps, cleaned, with roots removed
1 cup spinach
¾ cup shredded Parmesan cheese
½ cup fresh basil
¼ cup oil-cured sun-dried tomatoes
¼ cup unsalted butter, melted and cooled
1 teaspoon kosher salt
¼ cup plus 2 tablespoons olive oil

Combine all ingredients except the olive oil in a food processor. Turn processor on and slowly add oil. After all the oil is added, stop the processor and scrape sides to make sure all ingredients get incorporated. The pesto freezes well in an airtight container and will keep for 6 months.

Salt-Crusted Potatoes

French fries are a big hit in my kitchen, but oven-baked fries are typically a floppy disappointment, and frying is a commitment in time and cleanup that I'm not always game to take on. These potatoes are a good compromise between hot grease and a hot oven—they are crispy, salty, and as easy as simmering potatoes on the stove. Don't lose hope when you make them for the first time; they go from wet potatoes to salty potato nuggets about thirty seconds after the water evaporates. They pair nicely with ramp pesto and make a great side for chicken or beef.

SERVES 6

2 pounds small red potatoes or fingerlings
½ cup kosher salt

Place potatoes in a shallow saucepan large enough to accommodate the potatoes in a single layer on the bottom. Cover with water, add salt, and stir until salt dissolves. Bring to a boil over high heat. Reduce to a medium-low simmer and cook, stirring occasionally, until liquid has completely evaporated and potatoes are covered in salt, about 45 minutes. Serve with ramp pesto on the side as a dipping sauce.

Icebergs in May

IT WAS THE MIDDLE OF MAY. The snow was gone, our windows were free of their plastic wrap, and the *Karl*, our trusty mid-eighties brown speedboat, was back on the water. Summer was on its way, and we were forging ahead . . . into a lake dotted with icebergs.

The *Karl* came out of hibernation to ferry us across to Grant's Point and the South Channel for an iceberg photo safari. Meg, having watched *Titanic* for the first time the night before, kept a sharp lookout for any hull-ripping icebergs.

The shapes and colors of the icebergs were amazing—they were the perfect mirror to the blue sky and clouds overhead. Pieces of the frozen lake floated everywhere I looked; it was a completely new experience on this body of water that's so familiar to me. Each time we saw an iceberg cleave off a hunk of ice and release its water back to the lake, it was exhilarating. I felt blessed to be amidst the bergs, capturing their shapes, colors, and essence before they morphed into their summer form.

The summer solstice was about thirty days away—hard to believe, when the lake was barely above freezing and winter's ice sculptures were bobbing around in the water. I greet every summer with open arms, but a part of me would miss the starkness and hibernation of winter. The contrast of seasons played out against the canvas of Lake Superior is a sacred dance that's been going on for millennia, and I feel blessed to witness all of it—especially time-traveling pieces of winter dancing in the lake on May 17.

Summer

SUMMER IN BAYFIELD is all about beach days, fresh tomatoes, herbs from the garden, late dinners, sand in every crevice of the house, concerts at Big Top Chautauqua, strawberries, ice cream from the Candy Shoppe, boat rides among the Apostle Islands, weeding the garden, and wet dogs with joy in their hearts because they were just in the lake. We visit our garden like expectant parents, looking for the first bean, cucumber, pepper, or tomato of the season, and watch the boat slips and parking spots fill up with friends from the city.

Our long-awaited summer is the fun aunt, the season that gets all the attention, and the hoopla is warranted. Where else can you pick berries, take a ferry to an island, kayak to sea caves, hike to a waterfall, watch the sunset from the beach, climb a circular staircase to the top of a lighthouse, and jump off a sandstone cliff into Lake Superior in the space of a weekend? It's hard to beat the razzle-dazzle of a tourist town in the summer, and while I call Bayfield home, the "vacation" vibe is contagious. Seeing and hearing what visitors love about Bayfield reminds me how lucky I am to live in this little town.

Gathering
for the Table

FORAGING AND GATHERING: two words that have been lost in an increasingly noisy, busy, and disconnected world. Somewhere in the midst of our cold and white winter, my friend Ellen and I dreamed up a summer cooking and foraging class at her place, Blue Vista Farm, which she runs with her husband, Eric. Maybe it was our longing for the viscous summer evening light, the smell of soil warmed by the sun, or the varied shades of green in her field, but once the idea took hold, it was full steam ahead. There is something sacred in gathering food and preparing it for those you hold dear—it's our common ground and one that is the basis for community, healing, and our shared history.

Prior to meeting Ellen, I could have summed up my foraging experience in two words, *berry picking*, but she has opened a world full of wild and medicinal plants for me. I now know that cattails taste like clean lake water, sweet cicely tastes like anise and is a tonic for diabetes, and burdock root looks like the mandrakes from Harry Potter and is good for liver support.

The poet Mary Oliver said, "What about the sunflowers? What about the tulips, and the pines? Listen, all you have to do is start and there'll be no stopping." The world looks different when we realize we are surrounded by purpose and energy cloaked in green leaves, flowers, berries, bark, and roots. With our Gathering for the Table class, Ellen and I hoped to bring mindfulness back to the seemingly ordinary act of preparing a meal. There is life, humming and vibrating, in everything we eat, and the simple acts of recognition and gratitude change the way we look at what surrounds us—celebrating the sacred in the garden, the forest, and the farm.

As the evening wound down and we sat around the table, a familiar sated feeling settled in me. I looked around the table at the women whose hands and hearts had touched everything on my plate, at my son Will, whose spirit was in every image he captured that night, at Ellen and Eric, who have cultivated a farm bursting with growth and harvest, and I realized these are the blessings of bringing the sacred back to the table. When we gather around a table, we are performing a ritual that goes back to the beginning of time—a meal is a pause in our noisy world to connect with and nourish the people we love.

Summer Salad with Strawberries, Grilled Chicken, and Avocado

Bayfield is the perfect place to live if you like berries: strawberries, raspberries, and blueberries are plentiful here, and my kids gobble them up with abandon. The summer berry onslaught starts with strawberries, and we are big fans of North Wind Organic Farm and Rocky Acres Berry Farm in Bayfield. Both produce some of the sweetest strawberries I've ever tasted. Charlie looked at me last year after he had just devoured a pile of them and said, "Man, people who've never had a Bayfield strawberry have no idea what a strawberry should taste like." We eat them all day long—in smoothies and shortcakes, layered between angel food cake, on waffles, and in salads, which are a great idea when it is 150 degrees outside and you live in a hundred-year-old house without air-conditioning.

SERVES 6–8

FOR THE MARINADE AND CHICKEN

- ½ cup freshly squeezed lime juice
- ¼ cup tequila
- ¼ cup olive oil
- 4 garlic cloves, minced
- ¼ cup Tajin Clásico Seasoning
- 8 bone-in, skin-on chicken thighs

FOR THE CILANTRO LIME SALAD DRESSING

- 1 cup chopped cilantro
- ½ cup freshly squeezed lime juice
- ¼ cup orange juice
- 2 garlic cloves, minced
- 2 teaspoons Tajin Clásico Seasoning
- ¾ cup olive oil
  Salt and pepper to taste

FOR THE SALAD

- 6 cups chopped romaine
- 2 cups sliced strawberries
- 2 avocados, sliced
- ½ red onion, sliced
- ½ cup crumbled feta cheese (can substitute queso fresco)

Mix together all the marinade ingredients in a non-reactive bowl. Add the chicken pieces and marinate in the refrigerator for 4–6 hours.

Prepare a medium-hot gas or charcoal grill (350–400°F). Remove the chicken thighs from the marinade. Grill the thighs skin-side down until nicely browned, about 5 minutes. Flip the thighs and grill until they reach an internal temperature of 165°F, about 10 minutes longer. Transfer from the grill to a plate. Cover tightly and allow to rest while you prepare the salad dressing.

Place cilantro, lime juice, orange juice, garlic, and Tajin seasoning in a food processor or blender and combine. Slowly add olive oil until the dressing is emulsified. Taste and add salt and pepper if necessary.

After the chicken has rested, remove the meat from the bones and set aside. Place romaine, strawberries, avocados, red onions, feta, and chicken in a large bowl, add salad dressing, toss to combine, and serve.

Corn and Smoked Trout Chowder

One of the benefits of living in Bayfield is a nearly year-round supply of fresh and smoked fish from our local fishermen. I'm particularly fond of the brown sugar–cured smoked trout from Bodin's Fisheries, and this chowder is the perfect backdrop for all the smoky and sweet trout goodness. And an added bonus: this batch passed the "Meghan test." She's a bit of a chowder connoisseur and gave this one two thumbs up. High praise from my youngest daughter!

SERVES 6

6	ears of corn, corn kernels removed and cobs reserved
2½	cups whole milk
5	tablespoons butter
1	cup chopped red or orange bell pepper
1	cup sliced carrots
¾	cup chopped onion
½	cup chopped celery
¼	cup minced garlic
¼	cup flour
6	cups chicken stock (preferably home-made or low sodium)
3	cups diced red or Yukon potatoes
1	teaspoon Old Bay seasoning
1	teaspoon kosher salt, plus more to taste
¼	teaspoon cayenne
½	pound smoked trout, skinned, boned, and flaked
	Black pepper to taste

Place the corn cobs and the milk in a saucepan and simmer over low heat for 20 minutes. Remove the cobs from the milk and set pan aside to cool.

Melt the butter in a large heavy-bottomed stock pot or Dutch oven, then add bell pepper, carrots, onion, celery, and garlic and cook until softened, about 5 minutes. Stir in the flour and cook, stirring occasionally, for 3 minutes. Stir in the stock a little at a time and combine until the mixture is smooth. Add the potatoes, increase the heat, and bring to a boil; reduce the heat and simmer until potatoes are tender, about 10 minutes. Stir in the corn, Old Bay seasoning, 1 teaspoon salt, cayenne, and reserved milk, bring back to a boil, and then reduce to a simmer. Fold in the smoked trout. Simmer until heated through, 5–10 minutes longer. Add salt and pepper to taste, and serve immediately.

Thai Corn Chowder

Fresh corn is one of the sweetest parts of summer, and while grilled corn on the cob is everyone's favorite, this soup has earned a spot on my "What's for dinner after a day at the beach?" list. Corn, coconut milk, and Thai red curry paste combine for a spicy take on traditional corn chowder that has the added bonuses of taking about thirty minutes to pull together and not needing a hot oven.

SERVES 6

2   tablespoons coconut oil
½   yellow onion, diced
1   jalapeño, finely chopped
2   cloves garlic, minced
2   tablespoons grated fresh ginger
1   tablespoon Thai curry paste (I use Mae Ploy)
1   teaspoon fish sauce (I use Squid)
4   cups chicken stock (homemade or low sodium)
2   cups diced red potatoes
1   teaspoon kosher salt
4   cups corn kernels (fresh or frozen)
2   cans (13.5 ounces each) coconut milk
¼   cup fresh cilantro leaves
    Lime wedges, for serving

Place the coconut oil in a large heavy-bottomed stockpot or Dutch oven and melt over medium heat. Add the onions and jalapeño and cook until softened, about 10 minutes. Add the garlic, ginger, Thai curry paste, and fish sauce and cook for another minute or so. Add the chicken stock, potatoes, and salt and cook over medium heat until potatoes are tender, about 10 minutes. Add the corn, coconut milk, and cilantro and cook for 5 minutes over medium-low heat. Serve with lime wedges.

Watermelon Salad with Grilled Chicken and Feta

After a trip to Mexico, our friends Dana and Kathy brought us some Tajin, a mixture of Mexican chiles, lime juice, and sea salt, and it was love at first tangy bite. I immediately set out to use Tajin in as many dishes as I could dream up. Its spicy and tangy flavors are the perfect addition to my summer cooking repertoire, including this fresh take on grilled chicken. Sweet watermelon is the perfect foil for the spicy chicken, and the whole dish is even better when I add some salty Sassy Nanny Buttin' Heads feta.

SERVES 6–8

FOR THE SPICY BBQ GLAZE

- ⅓ cup packed brown sugar (light or dark)
- ¼ cup plus 1 tablespoon cider vinegar
- ¼ cup ketchup
- ¼ cup chili sauce
- 2 tablespoons Tajin Clásico Seasoning
- 2 teaspoons Frank's Hot Sauce
- 2 teaspoons Worcestershire sauce

FOR THE CHICKEN

- 8–10 bone-in, skin-on chicken thighs
- ¼ cup Tajin Clásico Seasoning

FOR THE DRESSING

- 1 cup olive oil
- 2 shallots, chopped
- ¼ cup minced garlic scapes
- ¼ cup chopped fresh mint
- ¼ cup chopped fresh oregano
- ¼ cup chopped fresh basil
- ¼ cup freshly squeezed orange juice
- ¼ cup freshly squeezed lime juice
- 2 teaspoons Tajin Clásico Seasoning
- ½ teaspoon agave or honey

FOR THE SALAD

- 4–5 cups arugula
- 2 cups cubed watermelon (rind removed)
- 1 cup crumbled Sassy Nanny goat feta or other feta cheese
- ½ red onion, thinly sliced
- ⅓ cup chopped cilantro

Mix all the BBQ glaze ingredients together in a medium bowl and set aside.

Gently loosen the skin of the chicken by sliding your fingers between the skin and meat; then, using your fingers, slide the Tajín under the skin. Sprinkle more on top for good measure and put the chicken, uncovered, in the refrigerator for 4 hours (the salt helps to dehydrate the skin and make it nice and crispy after it's grilled).

Prepare a medium-hot gas or charcoal grill (350–400°F). Grill the chicken thighs, flipping occasionally, until they reach an internal temperature of 165°F, about 20 minutes. Brush the glaze on the chicken about 5 minutes before you pull them off the grill; you want it to be caramelized but not burnt.

While the chicken is grilling, place all the dressing ingredients in a bowl and whisk to thoroughly combine. Assemble the salad ingredients. Shred the chicken and add to the assembled salad. Add dressing and toss to combine. Serve immediately.

Growing Up
among the Apostle Islands

SUMMER IS FAST AND FURIOUS in Bayfield, and when we find ourselves with a free afternoon, plenty of sun, and kids who are willing to hang out with their parents, we load up the boat and head out to the islands.

Lake Superior is a main character in countless Dougherty family stories, and I can't dream of a better way to raise our kids. We have traveled roughly ten thousand miles among the Apostle Islands, Isle Royale, and the Slate Islands, and those memories and experiences are the ballast that rights our ship when we lose our way.

We bought our first boat, a thirty-foot red sailboat named *Isle of Skye,* in 2000, and sailed into Bayfield the following summer. Ted's crew of one seasick wife, three small kids, and a 150-pound

Newfoundland dog named Guinness created chaos at times, but that first trip changed everything for us. Over the years, we've spent weeks traveling from island to island—building stick cities on Long Island, skipping rocks and looking for the hidden village on Michigan Island, and exploring the sea caves on Devil's Island.

It takes a certain kind of "out of the box" thinking to consider living on a thirty-foot sailboat with a pump toilet, an alcohol stove with an attitude problem, and at least one kid in diapers, but we had it in spades. The flies, temper tantrums (thrown by both kids and adults), Sadie vomiting from eating a pile of red licorice while we were under way to the Slate Islands, the Newfie vomiting up the plastic sand pail he ate on the dock on Stockton Island, and all the Matchbox cars, hairbrushes, towels, shoes, and pacifiers that were thrown overboard were worth it because every day there was at least one moment of wonder or joy. Like when two-year-old Charlie woke up in Washington Harbor on our first trip to Isle Royale, looked out the window, and saw his first moose. Or when eight-year-old Jack found "thunder rocks" near Loon Harbor in Ontario. Or when Sadie took her first steps on Isle of Skye. Or when Will jumped off the boat for the first time in Julian Bay in Stockton Island. Or when we had our first wood-fired sauna on Thompson Island near Thunder Bay. I never expected quiet perfection because I knew the good stuff always comes from the messy and brilliant business of living a life in a way that brings you to your knees with gratitude every now and then.

Now that the kids are pretty much grown, we don't have endless days to explore—and we have shorter, but no less magical, excursions on the lake. Thankfully, we are still out there, looking for a new chapter, coauthored by Lake Superior, to add to our family story.

Niçoise Salad in a Jar

Every week, a group of friends from around the Bayfield peninsula hop in their boats, armed with dinner and drinks, and spend a couple of hours on Long Island for happy hour and a bonfire. Charly, our stalwart leader, coined the phrase LICC (Long Island Cocktail Club), and it stuck. For a recent meeting, the boat was leaving the harbor at five-thirty sharp, and I needed to throw dinner together quickly. I always have Cento tuna, olives, potatoes, and eggs on hand. I made a simple vinaigrette, assembled the salad in lovely little jars, loaded up a cooler, and headed out to another beautiful summer night on the lake.

SERVES 8

FOR THE SALAD

- 8–12 fingerling potatoes
- 1 cup fresh green beans
- 1/3 cup olive oil
- 3 tablespoons preserved lemon, rinsed, pulp removed, and chopped (see recipe on page 35; you can substitute 1½ tablespoons grated lemon zest)
- 2 teaspoons Maldon sea salt
- 4 cans (3.5 ounces each) Cento tuna in olive oil
- 4 eggs, hard-boiled and sliced
- 2 tomatoes, chopped
- 3/4 cup pitted kalamata olives
- 1/4 cup salt-cured capers, rinsed
- 2 cups fresh spinach, washed and dried

FOR THE VINAIGRETTE

- 1/2 cup red wine vinegar
- 2 tablespoons finely minced shallot
- 2 tablespoons Dijon mustard
- 1/2 teaspoon salt, plus more to taste
- 1/4 teaspoon freshly ground pepper, plus more to taste
- 1/2 teaspoon chopped fresh thyme
- 1/4 teaspoon chopped fresh rosemary
- 1/2 teaspoon chopped fresh chives
- 1 cup good olive oil

Boil potatoes in salted water until fork tender. Wash and trim the green beans and steam until fork tender. Drain both well. While the potatoes and green beans are still warm, toss them with olive oil, preserved lemon, and sea salt.

Combine all ingredients for vinaigrette, except the olive oil, in a blender or food processor until well combined. Slowly add olive oil until the dressing is emulsified. Taste and add salt and pepper if needed.

Toss each salad ingredient (except spinach) with a little salad dressing and set aside. Don't use too much dressing; you want the salad components to be lightly dressed. Layer the salad ingredients in mason jars as follows: spinach, tomatoes, potatoes, green beans, eggs, spinach, tuna, olives, and capers. You can also arrange the salad on a large platter.

Chicken Kelaguen and Coconut Titiyas

Remember *The Brady Bunch?* And remember when they went to Hawaii, and Bobby found the voodoo doll, and all hell broke loose? Well, somewhere between Alice learning how to hula dance and the inevitable happy ending with a lesson, there was a luau. Since Ted and the boys were leaving for a canoe trip to the Boundary Waters on a Saturday morning (a luau-worthy expedition), I decided to channel my inner Alice, sans grass skirt, and make this chicken kelaguen, a Polynesian chicken salad, with sweet coconut flatbread.

SERVES 8–10

FOR THE KELAGUEN

- 1½   cups soy sauce or tamari
- 1½   cups cane vinegar
- ¾   cup pineapple juice
- ¼   cup Thai chili-garlic sauce (I use Huy Fong brand)
- 1   medium red onion, thinly sliced
- 3   pounds boneless, skinless chicken thighs
- 2   cups sliced green onions
- 1½   cups unsweetened grated coconut
- ¾   cup chopped fresh cilantro
- 2   jalapeños, minced
- ⅓   cup freshly squeezed lemon juice

FOR THE COCONUT TITIYAS

- 4   cups white flour, plus more for rolling out
- ¾   cup palm sugar (or ½ cup sugar)
- ½   cup butter, melted
- 2   teaspoons baking powder
- ¾   teaspoon kosher salt
- 1   can (13.5 ounces) coconut milk

Combine soy sauce, vinegar, pineapple juice, Thai chili-garlic sauce, and onion in a bowl. Add the chicken thighs and marinate for at least 8 hours or overnight.

Prepare a medium-hot gas or charcoal grill (350–400°F). Remove the chicken from the marinade and place on the grill, flipping once or twice, until completely cooked, about 10 minutes. Remove from grill, let cool slightly, and then cut into bite-sized pieces. Place the chicken in a bowl with the green onions, coconut, cilantro, and jalapeños. Mix to combine, pour the lemon juice over the top, and thoroughly mix again. Serve immediately or refrigerate, covered, for up to a day.

Combine flour, sugar, butter, baking powder, and salt in a large bowl and mix to thoroughly combine. Gradually add coconut milk until the dough starts to come together but isn't sticky (I used the entire can of coconut milk) and turn onto a floured surface. Knead until the dough is soft and pliable, 3–5 minutes, then cover and let the dough rest for about 30 minutes. Lightly flour a work surface. Separate the dough into individual golf-ball-sized pieces (about 18 to 20 pieces) and roll the dough balls into disks about 6 inches in diameter. Place a cast-iron skillet or grill pan on the stove and heat over medium-high heat. Place one piece of dough on pan at a time, and cover with the lid of a pan large enough to cover the entire piece. Cook until the bottom is browned and the top starts to puff and blister, 1 to 2 minutes. Flip it over and cook until lightly browned, another 1 to 2 minutes. Continue with remaining dough pieces. Allow to cool slightly and then serve with the chicken kelaguen. (Titiyas will keep, covered, for a day or so.)

Rich's Thai Fried Rice

I have a troubled track record with rice. Either I make too much, or it's not done, or it's a gluey mess. I bought a rice cooker, and while that's evened things out a bit in the "doneness" department, extra rice is a consistent problem. Or at least it was until Rich, Thai cooking whiz, came up to Bayfield a few summers ago with a sweet and spicy solution. Not only is this dish a good use of day-old rice, it highlights summer tomatoes, peppers, and onions. And it's also a quick dinner to throw together after a summer day on the lake—a little chopping, mincing, and sautéing gets dinner on the table in about thirty minutes.

SERVES 6–8

1	boneless, skinless chicken breast
1	teaspoon sesame oil
1	teaspoon cornstarch
3	tablespoons Golden Mountain Sauce (available at most Asian grocery stores or online), divided
5	tablespoons coconut oil, divided
2	eggs
4	cups day-old jasmine rice (freshly cooked rice doesn't work as well but can be substituted)
5	garlic cloves, minced
2	tablespoons minced fresh ginger
½	cup chopped sweet onion
1	red bell pepper, chopped
1½	cups bite-sized fresh pineapple chunks
2	tablespoons soy sauce
1	teaspoon raw sugar
1	teaspoon kosher salt
1	teaspoon Thai curry powder (available at most Asian grocery stores or online)
1	large tomato, sliced
¼	cup chopped green onion, white and green parts
½	cup cilantro

Cut chicken into bite-sized pieces and set aside. In a large bowl, combine sesame oil, cornstarch, and 1 tablespoon of the Golden Mountain Sauce. Add the chicken and marinate at room temperature for 15–20 minutes.

In a hot wok, heat 2 tablespoons of the coconut oil and scramble the eggs. Remove and set aside.

In another bowl, add remaining 2 tablespoons of Gold Mountain Sauce to jasmine rice and stir to combine. Set aside.

In the same wok, heat the remaining 3 tablespoons of coconut oil and melt over medium-high heat. Add the garlic and ginger and sauté for 15 seconds, then add the chicken (and whatever marinade is in the bowl) and cook for 2–3 minutes. Add the sweet onion and peppers; then add the pineapple. Stirring constantly, add the soy sauce, sugar, salt, and curry powder. Lower heat to medium and cook until the pineapple begins to release its juices.

Add the rice to the wok and break up any large pieces with your spatula. Stir until all ingredients are thoroughly combined. Remove from heat, add the tomato, green onions, and cilantro, and stir to combine. Serve immediately.

Campfire Dinner
on the Beach

IF WISCONSIN HAS A CLAIM TO FAME, right after the Packers and brandy old-fashioneds, a church basement fish fry is about as close to famous as it gets. On a very hot and muggy night in August, Charly's text came through inquiring about dinner at Bethesda Lutheran Church's fish fry in Bayfield. Given my complete lack of dinner motivation, a fish fry sounded pretty attractive . . . even if it was six-forty-five and the dinner ended at seven. Ted, Will, and I wrapped up our evening cocktail hour in the garden and headed down the street.

We walked in right as they were wrapping up but were served plates of lightly battered whitefish with homemade tartar sauce, complete with sweet pickle relish and buttered red potatoes sprinkled with parsley—a perfect Wisconsin fish fry. Just as perfectly Wisconsin were the two zip-top bags of fresh whitefish we walked out with. If there is one thing that typifies Bayfield, it's this: when you have more than you need, you share. We hiked home, baggies in hand, discussing who was going to skin the fillets.

It's not often that we have a free Saturday, but that coupled with some very un-northern-Wisconsin weather motivated us to head out of town to the beach that week-end. And since we had two plastic bags full of whitefish, dinner was already locked and loaded. We chose a beautiful and remote spot near Cornucopia. There was one wrinkle: the beach was accessible only by boat, and Ted had thrown out his back, which meant my daughter, Meghan, and her friend Emily were in charge of rowing. Despite spending every summer of her life on the water, Meghan had never rowed a boat, and Emily was a novice as well. The girls each grabbed an oar, and we started across the slough, backward. For some reason the boat wanted to go stern first, and every time we tried to turn the bow into the waves, we ended up traveling in circles. We embraced our backward boat and laughed, rowed, and circled our way to the beach.

The cabin is on a slip of land sandwiched between Bark Bay Slough and Bark Bay, and the contrast between the two shores is striking: the big lake meeting the horizon on one side and a slough with islands and cattails on the other. The kids grabbed the paddleboards and headed out on the lake, and I grabbed a cocktail and began the dinner prep.

I wasn't much of a Girl Scout, but I've had enough experience cooking dinner over a fire on the beach to know that aluminum foil is a mainstay. I had the building blocks for a campfire dinner: a fistful of herbs from the garden, some Sassy Nanny Buttin' Heads goat feta, butter, lemon, white wine, and a campfire. We sat by the fire, drank the rest of the wine, and watched the sun set behind Roman's Point.

Whitefish in Foil

This recipe is more a guideline than a hard and fast directive—kind of like an evening on the beach.

Skinned Lake Superior whitefish fillets
Butter
Lemons, quartered
White wine
Feta cheese
Garlic cloves, peeled and sliced
Fresh herbs (oregano, basil, thyme, rosemary, or whatever combination you have on hand)
Salt and pepper

Lay out two sheets of heavy-duty aluminum foil about 6 inches longer than your fillets and make a double-layer bottom. Place each fillet on foil and top with pat of butter (about a tablespoon), the juice of ¼ lemon, a splash of wine, about 3 tablespoons of crumbled feta, a few slices of garlic, a handful of herbs, and salt and pepper and cover with a third piece of foil (about the same size as the first two). Fold the aluminum sheets together, double or triple folding until you have a package a little larger than your fillet. Continue the process with additional fish.

Place the foil packets on the coals (double-layered foil side down) and cook for 10–12 minutes or so, depending on the temperature of the fire. Carefully open up a packet to check for doneness. The fish is done when it flakes easily with a fork.

Preserving
the Harvest

THE FUNNY THING about the harvest is that it's fast, furious, and at the time seemingly endless ... until the season ends. Then we're left with bushes and plants that are picked clean and mounds of fruits and vegetables in the kitchen ready to be preserved for the coming months of cold and snow. Food preservation is an age-old tradition and one that was born of an essential need to preserve the harvest when people had to rely on their own resources and planning to survive the winter. Today, with the focus on eating seasonally, preserving has more to do with keeping our pantries stocked with locally grown fruits and vegetables and extending the harvest than providing a lifeline between the growing seasons.

It can be hard to live and eat with the seasons. Strawberries from the grocery store in January aren't going to pass muster compared to the mason jar full of strawberries from Rocky Acres Berry Farm preserved as sweet jam on the shelf. And the resources needed to get those January strawberries to Bayfield are far greater than the cost to grow, pick, and package up Bayfield strawberries at the height of the season. Someone once told me that planting a garden is like growing your own money, and as my garden has grown and my food bill has shrunk, I've learned firsthand what they were talking about.

My first foray into preserving was as simple as freezing fruit in plastic bags—we would visit the local berry farms, pick buckets of fruit, place them in a single layer on a sheet tray in the freezer, and once the fruit was frozen, place it in a freezer bag and call it good. As my canning and preserving prowess has increased, I've expanded into marmalades, pickles, chutneys, and jams. There is great comfort in knowing you can control what you eat and how it's grown and prepared. Shelves full of preserved fruits and vegetables from gardens in my community create a food ethos that has everything to do with honoring the largesse of the earth and using it to nourish my family. For me, a stocked pantry in the middle of winter is the goal of preserving the harvest. And that desire to capture the abundance of our short growing season in Bayfield into glass jars goes back many generations—I'm just the new kid on the block.

Blueberry, Orange, and Ginger Jam

Judging from the bushes at Blue Vista Farm, it was a good year for blueberries. One warm August day, Sadie and Meghan and I picked over forty pounds, carted them home, and realized forty pounds is *a lot* of blueberries. We froze some, ate some, and then decided to make jam. Sounds easy, right? Boil some berries, add sugar and pectin, and call me Mrs. Smucker with my jars of jam in a row. We hit a few detours on the road to jam perfection, but after several phone calls to my mom (an experienced jam maker), a chance meeting at the IGA with the local jam guru, and some lucrative internet searches, we did end up with pretty little jars of jam in a row.

MAKES 8 HALF-PINT JARS

8	cups fresh blueberries
2½	cups sugar, divided
2	cups honey
2	packages (1.75 ounces each) Sure-Jell regular pectin
1	large orange
2	tablespoons minced crystallized ginger
1	tablespoon grated fresh ginger
½	teaspoon butter

Prepare jars and lids: place 8 half-pint jars on rack in a large pot, add enough water to cover the jars, and bring to boil over high heat. Boil for 10 minutes, then turn off heat and allow jars to rest in the hot water. Meanwhile, put bands and lids in small saucepan and cover with water. Heat over medium heat until the water is simmering, then remove pan from heat and allow bands and lids to rest in hot water until ready to use.

Working in batches if necessary, pulse blueberries in a blender until coarsely crushed. You should have about 6 cups.

Place 2¼ cups sugar and honey in one bowl. In another bowl, combine remaining ¼ cup sugar and pectin.

Zest and juice the orange. You should have about 2–3 tablespoons grated zest and ½ cup juice.

Combine blueberries, orange zest and juice, crystallized ginger, and grated ginger in large, heavy saucepan or stockpot. Stir in sugar-pectin mixture. Bring to a boil over high heat, stirring constantly.

Add sugar-honey mixture all at once. Stir in butter and return to a full rolling boil. Boil for 1 minute. Remove jam from heat and skim off any foam from surface.

Ladle hot jam into hot sterilized jars, leaving ¼-inch headspace. Wipe rims of jars, cover with lids, and screw on bands until just barely tight. Place jars on rack in pot and cover completely with water. Cover pot and bring to a boil over high heat. Boil for 10 minutes. Turn off heat, uncover pot, and allow jars to rest in water for five minutes. Remove jars from pot and allow them to rest undisturbed on countertop for 6 hours or overnight.

Note: Home canning carries food safety risks. For complete canning instructions, consult the University of Wisconsin Extension's many publications on home canning and preserving (http://fyi.uwex.edu/safepreserving) or the National Center for Home Food Preservation's resources (http://nchfp.uga.edu).

Strawberry and Lavender Balsamic Preserves

When Will joined the world of espresso drinkers, his beverage of choice was a lavender mocha. I love lavender in my garden, but I had tended to steer clear of it as a culinary herb. That same summer, my lavender plants were absolutely loaded with flowers, and I thought, if lavender's good with chocolate, it would be fantastic with strawberries, right? I did a quick internet search and stumbled upon a recipe for strawberry preserves with black pepper and balsamic vinegar—the perfect place to start. I monkeyed around with the recipe a little, added the lavender flowers and some pectin (a little gel-ing insurance), and the result was exactly what I hoped for: sweet and spicy with subtle lavender tones.

MAKES THREE 1-PINT JARS

4	cups washed, trimmed, and sliced strawberries
1	tablespoon fresh lavender flowers (or 1 teaspoon dried)
1	tablespoon Sure-Jell regular pectin
½	tablespoon butter
2	cups sugar
⅓	cup balsamic vinegar
1½	teaspoons coarsely cracked black pepper
½	teaspoon kosher salt

If you intend to can the preserves: Prepare jars and lids. Place three 1-pint jars on rack in a large pot, add enough water to cover the jars, and bring to boil over high heat. Boil for 10 minutes, then turn off heat and allow jars to rest in the hot water. Meanwhile, put bands and lids in small saucepan and cover with water. Heat over medium heat until the water is simmering, then remove pan from heat and allow bands and lids to rest in hot water until ready to use.

Combine the strawberries, lavender, and pectin in a large pan and bring to a boil. Keeping the mixture at a boil, add the butter and stir for 5 minutes, skimming any foam off the surface. Reduce heat to medium-low and add the sugar, balsamic vinegar, pepper, and salt and simmer until thickened, 30 to 40 minutes. Let cool completely and store in the refrigerator, covered, for up to a month or preserve it by canning it.

Canning instructions: Ladle hot preserves into hot sterilized jars, leaving ¼-inch headspace. Wipe rims of jars, cover with lids, and screw on bands until just barely tight. Place jars on rack in pot and cover completely with water. Cover pot and bring to a boil over high heat. Boil for 10 minutes. Remove jars from pot and allow them to rest undisturbed on countertop for 6 hours or overnight.

Note: Home canning carries food safety risks. For complete canning instructions, consult the University of Wisconsin Extension's many publications on home canning and preserving (http://fyi.uwex.edu/safepreserving) or the National Center for Home Food Preservation's resources (http://nchfp.uga.edu).

Red Pepper Jelly

I have a confession: I love hot pepper jelly spooned over cream cheese and served with Ritz crackers. And I have another confession: I had never served hot pepper jelly spooned over cream cheese because I wasn't sure where to procure the spicy jelly. Everything changed when I went to Northern Garden of Life near Ashland and saw a pile of smallish yellow peppers. Farm manager Jamie said they were hot (which was an understatement), and I grabbed a handful and headed home to create a little hot pepper jelly magic in my kitchen.

MAKES FOUR ½-PINT JARS

- 4 large red bell peppers, coarsely chopped
- 2 hot chiles (I use Hot Lemon Pepper variety), coarsely chopped
- 2 garlic cloves, chopped
- 3 cups sugar
- 1½ cups apple cider vinegar

Prepare jars and lids: Place 4 half-pint jars on a rack in a large pot, add enough water to cover the jars, and bring to boil over high heat. Boil for 10 minutes, then turn off heat and allow jars to rest in the hot water. Meanwhile, put bands and lids in small saucepan and cover with water. Heat over medium heat until the water is simmering, then remove pan from heat and allow bands and lids to rest in hot water until ready to use.

Pulse peppers and garlic in a food processor until finely chopped (be careful not to puree) and transfer to a medium heavy-bottomed saucepan. Add sugar and vinegar and bring to a boil. Reduce the heat and simmer until the peppers are reduced by two-thirds, about an hour.

Ladle hot jam into hot sterilized jars, leaving ¼-inch headspace. Wipe rims of jars, cover with lids, and screw on bands until just barely tight. Place jars on rack in pot and cover completely with water. Cover pot and bring to a boil over high heat. Boil for 10

minutes. Turn off heat, uncover pot, and allow jars to rest in water for 5 minutes. Remove jars from pot and allow them to rest undisturbed on countertop for 6 hours or overnight.

Note: Home canning carries food safety risks. For complete canning instructions, consult the University of Wisconsin Extension's many publications on home canning and preserving (http://fyi.uwex.edu/safepreserving) or the National Center for Home Food Preservation's resources (http://nchfp.uga.edu).

Indian Pickled Carrots

I've had a thing for pickles ever since I can remember; the salty tang of the brine and the crunch of the vegetables get me every time. My relative success at jam making and a taste of my friend Jill's pickled garlic scapes inspired me to try pickling. Since I am not a fan of floppy pickles, I decided to leave cucumber pickles for another day when I have more experience and many jars of successfully canned things under my belt. Carrots were a good place to start; they stand up to the heat of canning without turning to mush.

MAKES FOUR 1-PINT JARS

 3 cups apple cider vinegar
 1 cup raw sugar
 1 teaspoon salt
 2 tablespoons coconut oil
 ½ teaspoon fenugreek seeds
 ½ teaspoon brown mustard seeds
 ½ teaspoon fennel seeds
 ¼ teaspoon cumin seeds
 2 jalapeño peppers, thinly sliced
 2 cloves garlic, chopped
 1-inch-long piece of fresh ginger, peeled and finely minced
 1 pound carrots, washed and cut into uniform matchsticks
 ½ red onion, thinly sliced
 ¼ cup rough-chopped cilantro
 8 two-inch-long pieces of lime peel (2 for each container)
 1 cinnamon stick, broken into 4 pieces (1 for each container)

Prepare jars and lids: place 4 one-pint jars on rack in a large pot, add enough water to cover the jars, and bring to boil over high heat. Boil for 10 minutes, then turn off heat and allow jars to rest in the hot water. Meanwhile, put bands and lids in small saucepan and cover with water. Heat over medium heat until the water is simmering, then remove pan from heat and allow bands and lids to rest in hot water until ready to use.

In a medium-sized saucepan, heat the vinegar, sugar, and salt until the sugar is melted. Remove from the burner and set aside.

In a sauté pan, heat the coconut oil over medium-high heat until hot. Stir in the fenugreek seeds, mustard seeds, fennel seeds, and cumin seeds. Sauté until the spices are fragrant and then add the jalapeños, garlic, and ginger. Cook, stirring frequently, until ginger and jalapeño are soft, 2–3 minutes. Set aside.

Pack the sterilized canning jars with the carrots, onion slices, cilantro, lime peel, and cinnamon stick pieces. Divide the spice mixture among the jars and then pour the hot vinegar/sugar mixture over the contents, leaving ¼ inch of headspace. Wipe rims of jars, cover with lids, and screw on bands until just barely tight. Place jars on rack in pot and cover completely with water. Cover pot and bring to a boil over high heat. Boil for 10 minutes. Remove jars from pot and allow them to rest undisturbed on countertop for 6 hours or overnight. Store in a cool, dark, and dry place for at least 3 weeks before eating.

Note: Home canning carries food safety risks. For complete canning instructions, consult the University of Wisconsin Extension's many publications on home canning and preserving (http://fyi.uwex.edu/safepreserving) or the National Center for Home Food Preservation's resources (http://nchfp.uga.edu).

Tuscan Herb and Garlic Salt

About fifteen years ago, I decided to go big and make a full seven-rib prime rib for Christmas Eve dinner. Given the financial investment in all that beef, I wanted the results to be epic. And after an exhaustive search through my cookbooks and online, I determined the following: overcomplicating a beautiful piece of beef is a travesty and should be avoided at all costs. I settled on a simple Tuscan herb salt from one of my favorite cookery stores in Minneapolis, the Kitchen Window, and the prime rib was perfect in its simplicity.

After we moved to Bayfield, I was four hours away from the Kitchen Window's Tuscan salt, and since necessity (and an overabundance of fresh herbs in the garden) is the mother of invention, I set out to make my own herb salt. It is ridiculously easy to put together and an excellent way to preserve the summer herb bounty.

MAKES ABOUT 2 CUPS OF SALT MIX

2   cups coarse sea salt (do not use grey sea salt, as it's too oily)
3   cups mixed fresh herbs (thyme, basil, rosemary, lemon thyme, sage, tarragon—whatever you have on hand)
¼   cup fresh cracked pepper
5   cloves garlic, peeled

Place everything in the bowl of a food processor and blend until the salt is finely ground and green. Spread the salt on a sheet tray and let dry, uncovered, for a couple of days. Store in a covered container and use with wild abandon on anything and everything.

Everyone
Loves a Parade

BEFORE MOVING TO BAYFIELD I didn't have a lot of parade expertise outside of watching the Macy's Thanksgiving Day parade on TV as a kid. But I quickly learned that Madeline Island, two and a half miles across Lake Superior from Bayfield, puts on an old-fashioned red-white-and-blue extravaganza every Fourth of July that rivals gigantic Clifford the Big Red Dog balloons and super coordinated marching bands any day. The Madeline Island parade is a "come one, come all" kind of affair, and as long as you have costumes, a banner, a snazzy float, something to say, and a decent amount of candy to toss into the crowd, you're ready to roll. We recently traveled the length of the parade route with costumes, candy, and a Unimog with a message about clean water and cheap bacon.

Ted showed up with the Unimog a few years ago, the result of a trade with his cousin in Minneapolis. He left with his fully function-ing tractor and ATV and came home with an enormous, boxy military vehicle from the 1960s that was resolute in its commitment to remaining immobile, in spite of the change of ownership. Let's just say I wasn't a fan of the behemoth until I came home from the grocery store a few days before the parade and saw the happy pink pigs Ted had painted on the sides. It looked good.

We were geared up for fierce competition from our fellow parade participants, outfitting our-selves with costumes from a local production of *Animal Farm*, a huge bucket of candy, a bunch of kids, and juice boxes and Bloody Marys. We had a loosely choreographed plan: toss candy, hand out fact sheets, and chant "Farms Not Factories" every now and then. We made a respectable showing; we took second place, and our award (a recycled hockey trophy) is proudly displayed on top of the refrigerator. Next year, we're going to bust out some choreographed dance moves . . . that'll be a first place move for sure!

Grilled Moroccan Chicken Kebabs

My summer dinner repertoire requires judicious use of the oven and liberal use of the grill. As a result, Dougherty dinners mean lots of grilling outside when the house feels like a sauna inside. I made these flavorful kebabs for the first time when we were docked in Presque Isle Bay on Stockton Island over ten years ago, and when I make them now it takes me right back to that night. When those kebabs hit the heat, the aroma inspired a lot of conversation from our fellow boaters. The Moroccan spices are a little outside the norm, and the combination of preserved lemon, coriander, and cinnamon is really well suited to the dark meat of chicken thighs. There's nothing like a meal on a stick, and these kebabs make for a lovely summer dinner, on the beach or in your kitchen.

SERVES 6

FOR THE MARINADE

- ¼ cup olive oil
- ½ red onion
- 4 cloves garlic, peeled
  Peel of 1 preserved lemon (see recipe on page 35), thoroughly rinsed and chopped, pulp discarded
- 2-inch piece of fresh ginger, peeled and rough chopped
- 2 tablespoons thyme
- 2 teaspoons kosher salt
- 2 teaspoons cracked black pepper
- 1 teaspoon light brown sugar
- 1 teaspoon coriander
- 1 teaspoon cumin
- ½ teaspoon turmeric
- ¼ teaspoon cinnamon

FOR THE KEBABS

- 3 pounds boneless, skinless chicken thighs, cut into 2-inch pieces
- 2 red or yellow bell peppers, cut into 1-inch pieces
- 1 yellow onion, cut into 1-inch pieces
- 8 ounces white button mushrooms

FOR THE LEMON YOGURT SAUCE

- 2 cups plain Greek yogurt
- ½ cup chopped cilantro
- 3 tablespoons of reserved marinade
- 1 cucumber, peeled, seeded, and diced
- 6 green onions, white and light green parts, chopped
  Kosher salt and pepper

Place all the marinade ingredients in a food processor or blender and process until smooth. Reserve 3 tablespoons for the sauce. Put the chicken pieces in a bowl or a zip-top plastic bag and add the marinade. Mix to coat the chicken thoroughly with the marinade and place in refrigerator for 2–3 hours.

Prepare a medium-hot gas or charcoal grill (350–400°F). Remove chicken from marinade and set aside. Add the peppers, onions, and mushrooms to the marinade and stir to coat well. Skewer the chicken and vegetables and grill the kebabs over direct heat, turning the kebabs every 3–5 minutes, until the chicken is cooked thoroughly, about 15 minutes.

While the chicken is grilling, make the sauce. Combine the yogurt, cilantro, reserved marinade, cucumber, and green onions. Taste and add salt and pepper as needed; serve with the kebabs.

Bourbon Marinade Rib Eyes

I have raised a bunch of carnivores, and steak on the grill is a huge hit with the kids. A good piece of beef doesn't need much more than salt and pepper, but when I feel like getting a little fancy, I use this marinade. It's sweet and salty with a rich depth that complements beef particularly well. I like to cook these rib eyes in a cast-iron skillet set on the grill, which prevents flare-ups from the sugar in the marinade and the rendered fat as the steak cooks. Since you'll have some time because you won't be putting out fires, grab that open bottle of bourbon and a lowball glass, add some ice, and sit back and watch that steak cook. It's what all the cool grill-masters do while making dinner, seriously.

SERVES 4

½ cup soy sauce
½ cup bourbon
½ cup firmly packed dark brown sugar
2 tablespoons Dijon mustard
2 teaspoons seeded and minced jalapeño
2 garlic cloves, minced
1 teaspoon cracked black pepper
  Salt and pepper to taste
  Butter for the cast-iron pan
4 thick-cut beef rib eye steaks, bone-in or boneless

Combine the soy sauce, bourbon, brown sugar, mustard, jalapeño, garlic, and pepper in a medium bowl and whisk to combine. Place the steaks in a large zip-top plastic bag, add the marinade, seal the bag, and massage to cover the steaks with marinade. Place the steaks in the refrigerator and marinate for 8 hours or overnight.

Remove the steaks from the marinade, place on a platter, season with salt and pepper, and let them come to room temperature, 30 to 45 minutes. Preheat a gas or charcoal grill to high (about 450°F to 550°F). When the grill is ready, place a cast-iron skillet on the grates and allow to heat up for 5 minutes. Place about a tablespoon of butter in the pan, swirl it around, and then place the steak in the pan and cook, undisturbed, for 4 to 5 minutes. Flip the steaks, cover the grill, and cook until steaks are medium rare, about 4 minutes more. To check for doneness, use your finger to press on the meat: it should be firm around the edges but still give in the center. You can also use an instant-read thermometer; it should register between 130°F and 135°F. Transfer the steaks to a cutting board and let rest for at least 5 minutes before serving.

Alabama BBQ Chicken

Summer means all sorts of things in my kitchen, and one of the best things is that I can move my cooking outdoors to the smoker. I started smoking meat about twelve years ago, and I'm happy to report that beef brisket is no longer unfamiliar territory. But smoked chicken has a special place in my heart. It's where I started when I was new to the smoking world, and it's a great venue for my favorite BBQ sauce, a southern white BBQ sauce that I encountered when my husband's parents moved to Alabama. The combination of mayonnaise, cider vinegar, and horseradish is perfectly suited for chicken and is a nice change from the traditional tomato-based sauces common in the Midwest. It's a tangy and sweetish sauce that makes a mean coleslaw dressing as well as a kick-ass mop sauce for chicken and pork shoulder.

SERVES 8

12–14 chicken thighs and legs
⅓ cup Bad Byron's Butt Rub for seasoning chicken, plus 2 teaspoons for sauce (you can substitute your favorite BBQ spice rub)
1½ cups Hellman's mayonnaise
½ cup apple cider vinegar
⅓ cup horseradish
4 teaspoons sugar
½ teaspoon cayenne
2 garlic cloves, minced
2 cups wood chips or chunks, soaked for 1 hour in water (I use hickory wood chips)

Season the chicken thighs and legs on all sides with ⅓ cup of the spice rub and place, uncovered, in the refrigerator for at least 4 hours and up to 8 hours.

Mix the mayonnaise, vinegar, horseradish, sugar, 2 teaspoons BBQ rub (or use 1 teaspoon salt and 1 teaspoon pepper), cayenne, and garlic in a bowl, mix to combine, and place in refrigerator.

Preheat an electric smoker to 225°F and fill the smoker box with the wood chips/chunks. Place the chicken in the smoker and cook until the chicken reaches an internal temperature of 170°F, 3–4 hours. Transfer the chicken to a sheet tray and mop with the sauce. Cover and let stand for about 10 minutes. Serve immediately with extra sauce on the side.

Good Food
Grown by Good People

PETER, A DEAR FRIEND AND NEIGHBOR, walked into my kitchen and presented me with a bumper sticker from Penzey's Spices that said, "Love people. Cook them tasty food." I immediately placed it on our refrigerator (we have a tradition of plastering our refrigerator with stickers; it cuts down on having to wash the outside and gives guests something to read when they're waiting for dinner). Cooking and loving are intertwined in my kitchen, and while the tastiness factor is important, where the food comes from is key. And Northern Garden of Life, near Ashland, is nurturing a story of social justice cloaked in piles of tomatoes, squash, and peppers.

It took me a few years to find my way to Northern Garden of Life, but it was well worth the wait. One August I was looking for a pile of green beans to pickle and headed out with Charlie and Meghan to find the farm on Cherryville Road. We pulled through the gate and drove down a dirt road lined with row after row of vegetables: pumpkins, squash, potatoes, carrots, garlic, chard, tomatoes, beans, peppers, basil, and zucchini. I was in heaven.

The garden was started in 2009 by George Vernon, an Ashland businessman and farmer who had a deep appreciation for his community and believed that all people, especially those who frequented the Brick (a local food bank) deserved access to good, nutritious food. Over the past eight years the five-acre garden has donated well over thirty thousand pounds of fresh fruit and vegetables for the Brick, along with a significant portion of the garden's cash proceeds.

I've been to the garden many times since that first trip, and every time I've walked away thinking, *This is what food and farming are all about.* The prices are affordable, and they use a mixture of organic and sustainable growing practices that appeals to me. The quality and abundance of their produce is incredible: bin after bin of vegetables that hold the possibility of health, hope, and change for people who may not have access to good food.

Access to healthy food is the cornerstone of social justice and change. Many people don't have the means or opportunities to participate in the local food movement, and until there is space at the table for everyone, a sustainable and resilient food system won't take deep root and nourish the change we are seeking. The good people of Northern Garden of Life are planting seeds, cultivating soil, and harvesting their way to a more inclusive and fair future. George Vernon summed up his philosophy perfectly a couple of months before he passed away in 2012: "We just have to help people." I can't think of a better way to do that, one tomato at a time.

Tomato Jam

When tomato season is under way, it's all tomatoes, all day, and if you aren't on top of the garden's largesse, you'll soon be stacking them up everywhere. I was running out of good ideas until I looked at my shelf full of raspberry and strawberry jam . . . what if I concocted a tomato jam? After a few attempts that were less than stellar, this recipe came together amid the piles of tomatoes on my center island. It's the perfect anecdote to the Styrofoam tomatoes of January on my midwinter BLT. I'll schmear a couple of spoonfuls of this tomato jam alongside my mayonnaise, and I'll have a taste of summer tomato when it's snowing sideways outside my kitchen windows.

MAKES TWO 1-PINT JARS

2	teaspoons olive oil
1¾	cups rough-chopped red onion, divided
2	cloves garlic, minced
1	teaspoon kosher salt
½	teaspoon cracked black pepper
3	tablespoons brown sugar
4	cups diced tomatoes
¼	cup balsamic vinegar
½	teaspoon red pepper flakes
10	basil leaves, chopped
1	tablespoon chopped fresh thyme
1	tablespoon chopped fresh rosemary
	Salt and pepper to taste

If you intend to can the tomato jam: Prepare jars and lids. Place 2 one-pint jars on rack in a large pot, add enough water to cover the jars, and bring to boil over high heat. Boil for 10 minutes, then turn off heat and allow jars to rest in the hot water. Meanwhile, put bands and lids in small saucepan and cover with water. Heat over medium heat until the water is simmering, then remove pan from heat and allow bands and lids to rest in hot water until ready to use.

Heat olive oil in a medium, heavy-bottomed saucepan over medium-high heat. Add 1½ cups onion, garlic, salt, and pepper. Reduce the heat to low and cook, stirring often, until the onions are softened and starting to turn golden brown, about 20 minutes.

Stir in the brown sugar and then add the tomatoes, vinegar, and red pepper flakes. Simmer, uncovered, until the mixture is thick and has a jamlike consistency, about 1 hour.

Remove half of the tomato jam from the saucepan and use an immersion blender to puree the remaining half in the saucepan. Add the reserved jam back to the saucepan and add the basil, thyme, rosemary, and remaining onions. Simmer for another 15 minutes, then taste and add salt and pepper as needed. Store covered in refrigerator for a month or preserve the tomato jam by canning it.

Canning instructions: Ladle hot jam into hot sterilized jars, leaving ¼-inch headspace. Wipe rims of jars, cover with lids, and screw on bands until just barely tight. Place jars on rack in pot and cover completely with water. Cover pot and bring to a boil over high heat. Boil for 20 minutes. Remove jars from pot and allow them to rest undisturbed on countertop for 6 hours or overnight.

Note: Home canning carries food safety risks. For complete canning instructions, consult the University of Wisconsin Extension's many publications on home canning and preserving (http://fyi.uwex.edu/safepreserving) or the National Center for Home Food Preservation's resources (http://nchfp.uga.edu).

Fresh Tomato Pasta Sauce

Garden-fresh tomatoes are one of my favorite parts of summer in Bayfield, and I have to admit, I'm a bit of a tomato hoarder. I have two raised beds devoted entirely to tomatoes, and yet I'm a frequent farmers' market customer with a basket full of cherry, grape, Roma, and heirloom varieties. When it comes time to cook all those tomatoes, I'm a believer in letting the tomato shine, and this pasta sauce is definitely tomato-centric. It's good on pasta, broiled whitefish, and grilled chicken thighs, or as a bruschetta topping on grilled baguette slices.

SERVES 6

⅓ cup extra-virgin olive oil (use the highest quality available)
2 tablespoons seeded and minced jalapeño
5 cups ripe cherry tomatoes, stemmed and halved
2 cloves garlic, minced
1 teaspoon finely grated lemon zest
3 tablespoons chopped fresh basil
3 tablespoons butter
Salt and pepper to taste

Heat oil in a large sauté pan over medium-high heat. Add the jalapeño and cook, stirring often, until soft, 2–3 minutes. Lower the heat to medium, add the tomatoes, and cook, stirring often, until they begin to burst and release their juice, 6–8 minutes. Add the garlic and cook for another 30 seconds or so, then add the lemon zest and stir to combine. Remove the pan from the heat, add the basil and butter, and gently stir to combine. Add salt and pepper to taste and serve immediately.

Roasted Carrot, Feta, and Mascarpone Pizza

When life gives you a seemingly endless supply of carrots, a little creative thinking is called for. There's nothing like walking out to the garden, picking what's ready to eat, and assembling it into dinner. It's kind of like putting a puzzle together with pieces from my garden.

MAKES TWO 12-INCH PIZZAS (but the dough recipe makes enough for up to 7 pizzas, and it freezes well)

FOR THE PIZZA DOUGH

- 3 cups warm water
- 1/3 cup olive oil
- 1½ tablespoon yeast (I use SAF red instant yeast)
- 1½ tablespoons kosher salt
- 1 tablespoon sugar (white or raw)
- 7 cups bread flour

FOR THE PIZZAS

- 2–3 carrots, peeled and sliced lengthwise into 3- or 4-inch pieces (about 10–12 pieces)
- 2 tablespoons olive oil
  Salt and pepper to taste
- 1 cup crumbled feta
- 2/3 cup mascarpone
- 1 clove garlic
- 2 tablespoons chopped fresh oregano
- 1 teaspoon freshly grated lemon zest
- 1/2 teaspoon red pepper flakes
- 1/4 red onion, thinly sliced
- 1/4 cup rough-chopped oil-cured olives

To make the dough, combine the water, oil, yeast, salt, and sugar in a large bowl or the bowl of a stand mixer. Add the flour and mix until it comes together, about 3 minutes using the dough hook of the stand mixer, longer if mixing by hand. Knead for 5 minutes (with stand mixer or by hand); cover loosely and allow to rest at room temperature until the dough doubles in volume, about 2 hours.

When ready to assemble the pizzas, preheat the oven to 400°F and line a sheet tray with parchment paper. Toss the sliced carrots with the olive oil and salt and pepper to taste and place on the tray. Roast until tender, about 30 minutes. Set aside (the carrots can be prepared in advance and stored in the refrigerator until ready to use).

Combine the feta, mascarpone, garlic, oregano, lemon zest, and red pepper flakes in the bowl of a food processor and process until smooth.

Raise the oven temperature to 450°F and place a pizza stone in the oven. Heavily flour a work surface. Remove a tennis ball–sized piece of dough from the larger ball and roll it out into a 12-inch round on work surface. Using a fork, poke holes in the crust. Transfer the crust onto a pizza peel or a parchment-lined baking sheet without a lip. Spread about half of the feta/mascarpone mixture on the crust and then layer roasted carrots, red onions, and olives on top. Repeat with another ball-sized piece of dough and remaining toppings to make a second pizza. Wrap remaining dough tightly and freeze up to 3 months.

Carefully place the pizza on the pizza stone and bake until the edges of the crust are brown and the onions are beginning to brown, about 10 minutes. Remove from the oven and serve immediately.

Corn Man

WE HAVE MANY SIGNS OF SUMMER IN BAYFIELD. The Candy Shoppe is open until nine P.M., parking spots on Rittenhouse are few and far between, farmers' markets are in full swing, and the Corn Man cometh from Baronett, Wisconsin. I encountered Baronett Bob, or Corn Man as he's known in Bayfield, about thirty years ago in Cumberland, Wisconsin, where Ted's parents had a cabin. For about a month or so every summer, there'd be a pickup truck parked at the corner gas station with a big red and white SWEET CORN sign. Little did I know then that so many years later we'd be enjoying the same corn sold by the now locally famous Corn Man in Ashland.

Starting in August, Bob parks at the Pure Dairy parking lot on US Highway 2 Monday through Saturday, eleven-thirty until six or until the corn is gone. He got into the corn and produce business—also raising cabbages, cucumbers, and tomatoes—in 1982 or thereabouts. He grew up on a dairy farm and was in a bit of a transitional mode. His father asked him if he wanted to buy more cows, and he said, "No, I want to grow sweet corn." And he's been at it ever since. His corn has twice the water content of average sweet corn and can be eaten on the spot, he boasts.

Resting his feet "just a bit" as he sits in the back of his farm truck, he trades bags of corn for five-dollar bills to a steady stream of customers.

"There's a few secrets," he says. "Some I will tell you. Some I won't."

1. Test many varieties, he says. Bob has experimented with three hundred. His favorite so far is his latest, a variety he's calling Bob's Secret Super Sweet Corn.

2. Pick it fresh each day. "Some people who sell corn don't even grow the corn," he says. "They pull it off a huge truck with corn that's been sitting for a while."

3. Pick the sweet corn in its prime.

"There's more," he says. "But that's all I'm going to tell you."

As long as he keeps showing up in the Pure Dairy parking lot and selling us his super sweet corn, he can keep all the secrets he wants. I just want his corn.

Summer Quiche with Tomatoes and Sweet Corn

Nothing says summer like bags of Ashland's Corn Man corn, freshly shucked, and a kitchen full of tomatoes in various shades of green, yellow, and red. Quiche is a quick and easy dinner option, and since breakfast for dinner is a Dougherty family favorite, it was a no-brainer as I stared into the refrigerator late one afternoon, looking for inspiration. This quiche really shines when made with garden-fresh tomatoes and sweet corn; although it won't be as good with grocery store tomatoes, it's still delicious.

SERVES 8

- 1 9-inch pie crust (homemade or store-bought)
- 2 teaspoons butter
- 3 ears peak-season sweet corn, kernels sliced off cobs (about 2½ cups)
- 1 cup whole milk
- 1 cup heavy cream
- 3 corncobs (optional)
- 3 large eggs
- 1 teaspoon salt
- ½ teaspoon black pepper
- ½ cup crumbled cooked pancetta or bacon
- ½ cup crumbled Gorgonzola
- 2 pounds assorted garden-ripe tomatoes, cut into ½-inch slices (about 2 cups)

Preheat oven to 350°F. Roll out the crust and fit into a 9-inch pie pan, nonstick cake pan, or fluted tart pan. Set a large piece of parchment paper on top of the crust and fill with dried beans. Bake crust for 10 minutes. Remove beans and parchment and set crust aside.

In a Dutch oven, heat butter over medium heat. When butter is melted, stir in the corn kernels. Sauté, stirring occasionally, for 5 minutes. Add the milk, cream, and corncobs, if using, to the Dutch oven. Increase heat to high and bring the mixture to a boil; reduce heat to low and simmer for 20 minutes.

Remove from the heat, discard the corncobs, and allow to cool for 15 minutes. Place a food mill fitted with the fine disc over a medium bowl.

In a blender, puree the corn and cream mixture (use caution if the mixture is still hot). Pour the pureed corn and cream into the food mill and begin to push the corn though the food mill. Measure out 2 cups of the corn/cream mixture and put it in a medium bowl; add to it the eggs, salt, and pepper and whisk to combine.

Sprinkle the pancetta and Gorgonzola over the bottom of prepared crust. Pour egg mixture into crust and arrange tomato slices over the top of the egg mixture. Bake until edges of crust are golden brown and center of quiche is just set, 40–45 minutes. Cool on a wire rack for 15 minutes before serving.

Raspberry Island
Light

TO OUR SURPRISE, THE BAYFIELD CHAMBER OF COMMERCE called and inquired about the Dougherty clan participating in a commercial about the Apostle Islands for the Wisconsin Department of Tourism. To be fair, there aren't many families with five kids who live in Bayfield, have a boat, and are familiar with the Apostle Islands; the playing field was pretty sparsely populated when it came to finding local color. We are always game for an adventure, so we agreed to share our love of the Apostle Islands, on camera with people we've never met, on a sunny summer morning.

F. Ross Holland, author of *Great American Lighthouses,* said, "Within the boundaries of the Apostle Islands National Lakeshore is the largest and finest single collection of lighthouses in the country," and the Raspberry Lighthouse is a cornerstone of that collection. It's a busy place in the summer (ten thousand people visit each year), and since we tend to stick to beaches and islands that are off the beaten path, it's been a long time since we've been out there. The lighthouse, along with its outbuildings and grounds, have been extensively renovated in the last ten years, and it has certainly earned its "Showplace of the Apostles" title. The gardens, the croquet court, the boathouse, and the furnishings in the keeper's quarters are beautiful, re-created with a remarkable attention to detail.

The United States Congress appropriated $6,000 in 1859 to build the lighthouse at the urging of Henry Rice, founder of Bayfield, because shipping traffic was increasing in the West Channel. The Raspberry Island light was the third lighthouse built in the Apostle Islands, behind Michigan Island in 1857 and Long Island in 1858. The lighthouse and keeper's quarters were completed in 1862 and officially opened in July 1863 when the Fresnel lens arrived from France and was installed. The lighthouse was renovated and expanded to accommodate assistant keepers and their families in 1906 and then decommissioned in 1947 when it was converted to an automatic operation. The Fresnel lens stayed in the area, though; it was donated to the Madeline Island Museum around 1960.

While we were waiting for our fifteen minutes of fame with the film crew, we walked around the grounds, and Charlie remarked that not much has changed since the first keeper moved in over 150 years ago. As I stood on the lawn, looking at the lake, I realized he was right: the Apostle Islands and its lighthouses are living reminders of the rich heritage of brave men and women who chose to live far from the comfort provided by cities and the mainland. The Apostle Islands are a living history museum, and reacquainting myself with the history that lives beside me is a good reminder of how lucky we are to live in Bayfield.

Peter's Gazpacho

Gazpacho is an uncooked soup that at its best tastes like summer in a bowl and at its worst tastes like a salsa smoothie. A good one, with a baguette and good butter on the side, is about as close as you'll come to a perfect meal on a hot summer evening. So, when Peter, a good friend and good cook, made gazpacho and invited us for dinner, I knew it was going to be fantastic. His mom got the recipe from the *LA Times* in the late '70s, and he's been making his adapted version of it for years. I like to serve bowls of this topped with a dollop of sour cream seasoned with chopped cilantro, minced garlic, and lime juice.

SERVES 6

4	cups V8 vegetable juice
1	cup peeled, diced, and seeded tomato
1	can Ro-Tel Original Diced Tomatoes and Green Chiles
½	cup diced onion
½	cup peeled, diced, and seeded cucumber
½	cup minced celery
½	cup minced red bell pepper
⅓	cup minced cooked carrots
¼	cup chili sauce
2	tablespoons red wine vinegar
2	tablespoons olive oil
1	clove garlic, minced
2	tablespoons minced fresh tarragon
1	tablespoon minced fresh basil
1	tablespoon minced fresh cilantro
1	tablespoon freshly squeezed lime juice
1	tablespoon Worcestershire sauce
2	teaspoons minced fresh parsley
1	teaspoon salt, plus more to taste
½	teaspoon ground mace

Combine everything in a large pot and stir well. Cover and place in the refrigerator for a couple of hours to let the flavors develop. Taste and add salt if necessary before serving. Serve cold.

Thai Watermelon Gazpacho

SERVES 6

6   cups seeded and chopped watermelon, pureed in a blender
2   cups seeded and finely diced watermelon
2   cups diced fresh tomatoes
1   peeled and seeded cucumber, diced small
1   yellow pepper, seeded and diced small
    Kernels cut from 2 ears of sweet corn, cooked
1   garlic clove, minced
1   small jalapeño, seeded and minced
½   red onion, minced
¼   cup plus 2 tablespoons freshly squeezed lime juice
¼   cup chopped fresh cilantro leaves and stems
¼   cup minced fresh ginger

2½ tablespoons chopped fresh Thai basil (can substitute Italian basil)
1½ tablespoons fish sauce
1   teaspoon kosher salt, plus more to taste
    Pepper to taste
1   avocado, sliced, for serving

In a large bowl, combine all ingredients except avocado; taste and add salt and pepper as needed. Refrigerate for at least 1 hour; serve cold with avocado slices on top.

Happy Cows **in Mellen**

Good farmers, who take seriously their duties as stewards of Creation
and of their land's inheritors, contribute to the welfare of society in more ways than society
usually acknowledges, or even knows. These farmers produce valuable goods, of course;
but they also conserve soil, they conserve water, they conserve wildlife, they conserve open
space, they conserve scenery.

—Wendell Berry, *Bringing It to the Table:*
Writings on Farming and Food

I OWE MY INTRODUCTION TO THE O'DOVERO-FLESIA FARM to my quest for a seriously good
hot dog. My preferred hot dog supplier, a meat market in Mellen, exited the sausage business a few
years ago, and while Hebrew Nationals are a good substitute, they just aren't the same. Everything
changed when my friend Pete told me about the O'Doveros' cattle farm and meat market—I was
back in all-beef, natural-casing hot dog heaven. And, lucky for me, O'Dovero-Flesia farmstead also
included dry-aged beef, the perfect pork belly for pancetta, and a picturesque collection of dairy cows,
beef cattle, buildings, and pastures.

Five generations of O'Doveros have called these thousand acres at the base of the Penokee Hills home, and as I pulled into the driveway, I could understand why: it's beautiful. Framed by a mixed hardwood and pine forest, the undulating pastures blend into the rising Penokee Hills. Two barns with fieldstone foundations (built in the late 1920s or early 1930s) wear the weathered patina of ninety-some years of Wisconsin rain, wind, snow, and sun.

Monica Vitek, the matriarch of the clan, has the commanding presence that only years of nurturing and no-nonsense mothering can provide. Her grandparents, Emmanuel and Monica, emigrated from Turin, Italy, to Mellen in the early 1900s to work in the Mellen tannery. That business opened in 1896 and was the largest and most productive tannery in the country, in part because of the abundance of hemlock trees in the region (the tanning process relied on hemlock bark). For twenty-six years the tannery employed many Italian immigrants who came to northern Wisconsin to work and set down roots. When a new chemical process was introduced in 1922, the tannery shut down. Most of the men went to Hurley to work in the iron mines or to Kenosha to find factory work. Emmanuel, however, decided to stay in Mellen and bought the farm in 1926.

Emmanuel and Monica passed the farm to their children, who passed it to theirs, and so on down the line. The family's stewardship and pride in the farm is evident. As I sat down to have lunch with Monica, her husband, Poppy, and their daughter, Wendy, Monica spoke of her father. She said he always told her, "You never take more from the land than what you put back, plus a little extra," and of the 155,000 trees he planted in his lifetime to ensure the family didn't deplete the forest.

We laughed about chasing heifers, cousins weeding the cornfield (after they complained of boredom), "eating your way to bed" on Christmas Eve, and stacking wood with surly teenagers. Monica offered to teach me how to make bagna cauda, a dish she made with her mother; Wendy came up from the basement with a jar of homemade antipasto from last summer's garden; and there was a hunk of Asiago in my hands as I was leaving. Their generosity of spirit and pride in the farm they've called home for five generations was inspiring. The extraordinary (or not, depending on how you look at it) thing is it's still a working farm—raising cattle and supporting a family who are rooted in this place as much as the trees are rooted in the hillside.

Family farms are a rarity in this age of agribusiness and large-scale feeding operations, and a farm like the O'Doveros' is important. Farmers remind us that good land management practices and animal husbandry are vital to the health of a community. They are the conservationists of our time.

Homemade Corn Dogs

What's better than a hot dog from the O'Doveros? An O'Dovero hot dog dipped in batter, fried in a cast-iron skillet, and eaten with a schmear of good mustard. I'm a picky corn dog connoisseur (if there is such a designation), and the only corn dog worth eating is hand-dipped in batter—trust me, I've done a fair amount of market research. I grew up in a family of devout Minnesota fairgoers, and I earned my carnival food chops through good old-fashioned trial and error. These corn dogs passed muster with flying colors!

MAKES 12 CORN DOGS

3   cups pancake mix (I use Krusteaz)
1   cup yellow cornmeal
1   whole egg, slightly beaten
1   cup buttermilk
1   cup water, plus more if needed
    to thin batter
    Canola or vegetable oil, for frying
12   all-beef, natural-casing hot dogs
    Chopsticks

In a large bowl, combine pancake mix and cornmeal. Stir to combine. Add egg and buttermilk. Add 1 cup water and stir, adding more water as needed for the batter to become slightly thick but not overly gloopy.

Pour vegetable or canola oil into a large cast-iron skillet to a depth of ¾ inch and heat over medium-high heat to 375°F. Drop in a bit of batter to see if it's ready; the batter will immediately start to sizzle but should not immediately brown or burn.

Insert sticks into hot dogs lengthwise so they're two-thirds of the way through. Pour the batter into a large drinking glass or quart-sized canning jar. Dip the hot dogs into the batter and allow excess to drip off for a couple of seconds. Cooking two corn dogs at a time, carefully drop them into the oil (stick and all) and use tongs or a spoon to make sure they don't hit the bottom and stick. Using the tongs, rotate to ensure even browning, and cook until the batter is deep golden brown, about 4–5 minutes. Remove from the oil, place on a rack or paper towel–lined sheet tray to drain. Continue with remaining corn dogs.

Adapted from the Pioneer Woman,
www.thepioneerwoman.com

Spicy Beer Mustard

You know things are getting bad when your son opens the refrigerator, looks at you, and says, "All we have to eat are condiments and butter." Some might say I'm a condiment hoarder, and I've recently taken it to the next level—not only am I hoarding, I'm creating. Ever since I made my first batch two years ago, store-bought mustard just doesn't . . . cut the mustard. For instance, I just fried up a batch of homemade corn dogs, and regular old French's yellow mustard pales in comparison to all that deep-fried goodness. However, freshly made spicy beer mustard is not only up to the task, it takes a corn dog to a whole new level. And the good news about all this corny mustard love is that making your very own batch is about as easy as chopping, mixing, and stirring. In less than a week, you'll have a bracing batch of spicy beer mustard and you can start your own condiment collection. It's a slippery slope, condiment hoarding, but it's a good ride.

MAKES ABOUT 4 CUPS OF MUSTARD

1½   cups dark beer
½   cup brown sugar
5   tablespoons honey
1½   cups apple cider vinegar
2   garlic cloves, finely minced
1   shallot, finely minced (about 1 tablespoon)
1   teaspoon turmeric
½   teaspoon minced rosemary
½   teaspoon minced fresh thyme
¾   cup brown mustard seeds
¾   cup yellow mustard seeds
1   cup dry powdered mustard (I use Colman's)

In a medium saucepan over medium heat, combine the beer, brown sugar, and honey and heat until sugar and honey are dissolved. Remove from the heat and add the vinegar, garlic, shallot, turmeric, rosemary, and thyme. Stir to thoroughly combine and set aside until it has cooled to room temperature. Add the brown and yellow mustard seeds, mix well, and place in a covered glass jar. Let it sit at room temperature, stirring a few times a day, for 2 to 3 days. Place the mixture in a blender with the mustard powder and blend until smooth. Cover and refrigerate overnight before serving. Mustard will last several months in the refrigerator.

Long Island Farewell

IT WAS A BIG DEAL WHEN JACK, our oldest son, moved to Madison to start his next chapter as a freshman Badger. And such a momentous occasion called for a stellar party. Shrimp boils are a Dougherty family favorite with enough wow factor to send Jack off to Madison with Bayfield flair. On a perfect August afternoon, we loaded up the *Karl* with shrimp, green beans, a bucket of spices, potatoes, and beer and headed to Long Island to celebrate the kid who for nineteen years had brought so much joy, pride, laughter, and love into our lives.

We couldn't have asked for a better afternoon: no bugs, a sun-soaked beach, warm water, dear friends, and a boiling kettle of spiced water, shrimp, and Corn Man corn. It's hard to put into words what it felt like, knowing that in seven days we would be driving Jack to Madison and leaving him there, in a dorm with six thousand other freshmen. It was the kind of joy with a sharp edge that made me catch my breath and blink back tears because I understood for the first time what bittersweet really means. Jack was taking his first steps toward independence and away from us, but the tapestry we've woven together from nights like these will always be his connection to home and the people who love him.

One of our friends, Teddy, gave Jack Edward Abbey's wise words for a happy life.

Do not burn yourselves out. Be as I am—a reluctant enthusiast . . . a part-time crusader, a half-hearted fanatic. Save the other half of yourselves and your lives for pleasure and adventure. It is not enough to fight for the land; it is even more important to enjoy it. While you can. While it's still here. So get out there and hunt and fish and mess around with your friends, ramble out yonder and explore the forests, climb the mountains, bag the peaks, run the rivers, breathe deep of that yet sweet and lucid air, sit quietly for a while and contemplate the precious stillness, the lovely, mysterious, and awesome space. Enjoy yourselves, keep your brain in your head and your head firmly attached to the body, the body active and alive, and I promise you this much; I promise you this one sweet victory over our enemies, over those desk-bound men and women with their hearts in a safe deposit box, and their eyes hypnotized by desk calculators. I promise you this; You will outlive the bastards.

As I watched Jack shake Teddy's hand, I knew everything was exactly as it should be. Jack was ready to move on, I was ready to let him go, and we've been blessed with a lifetime of gratitude—for our family, friends, countless memorable dinners, and the lake and beaches that are the backdrop to our story.

As the night wound down and the full moon rose over the South Channel, I took a minute to take it all in. I knew we'd be on this beach again, but it would be different next time. I wanted to remember every last moment of it: Charlie's face when the boil hit the table, Jack filling up a Corona bottle with sand to take to Madison, Meghan triumphantly hoisting the paddle overhead when she saw me on the beach, and Will walking down the beach, camera in hand, to catch the sunset. On that August night, I couldn't have been happier.

As with all good parties, time flew by, and before we knew it, the sun had set, the boats were loaded, and we were on our way back to Bayfield. Until my friend Kathy had a brilliant idea: a moonlit swim in the South Channel. We stopped the boats, jumped into the water, and spent ten minutes swimming under the luminescent moon. It was the perfect end to a beautiful night—immersed in the water, preparing to cross a new threshold in our family story,

Low Country Shrimp Boil

SERVES 10

6 quarts water
3 cups beer
²/₃ cup seasoned salt
¹/₃ cup kosher salt
¹/₄ cup black peppercorns
¹/₄ cup dried parsley
¹/₄ cup yellow mustard seeds
¹/₄ cup dill seeds
¹/₄ cup cayenne
5 tablespoons Worcestershire sauce
2 tablespoons celery seeds
2 tablespoons coriander seeds
2 tablespoons whole cloves
1 tablespoon plus 2 teaspoons Frank's Hot Sauce
1 tablespoon whole allspice
1 tablespoon crushed red pepper flakes
10 cloves garlic
3 lemons, quartered
2 jalapeños, quartered and stems removed
2 onions, quartered
18 new potatoes
6 ears of corn, broken in half
3 pounds of shell-on shrimp

In a large pot, combine all ingredients except potatoes, corn, and shrimp. Bring to a rapid boil and boil for 15 minutes.

Add potatoes and boil for 15 more minutes. Add corn and boil for 5 more minutes.

Turn off heat, add shrimp, and cover pot. Let stand, stirring a couple of times, until shrimp is pink and cooked through, 3–5 minutes. Drain and serve immediately.

Sunday at Stockton

THERE IS NOTHING LIKE A LATE-SUMMER SUNDAY spent on Lake Superior. It's quiet, beautiful, and restorative. Well, as quiet as a boat full of Doughertys can be. We went to the north end of Stockton and spent the afternoon sitting on the rocks, watching the kids jump off the boat and swim. It was as good as a summer afternoon can get.

When we bought our trawler, *Talisker,* fourteen years ago, Charlie was in diapers, Sadie was four years old, and I was pregnant with Meg. Leaving the dock meant vigilant monitoring of the kids' whereabouts and the constant zipping and unzipping of life jackets. On this trip, I sat up in the flybridge with Ted on the way over, reading a magazine. Time moves fast, and you have to be ready for the ride.

I had grabbed some leftovers for our lunch and made a salad on the way over. Grilled chicken thighs, spinach, red peppers, and avocados with fresh lime juice and Tajín seasoning—delicious, but the chips and Oreos were a bigger hit. That's the way it goes when your target lunch audience is fourteen and under. (However, Zeus the dog loved the salad.)

As we headed home, I thought about all the miles we have traveled together—Isle Royale, the Slate Islands, Loon Harbor, Grand Marais, Thunder Bay, the Apostle Islands. What a gift to have memories of safe harbors, northern lights, wild blueberries, sandy beaches, thunder rocks, and saunas as part of our family tale. Moving to Bayfield has had its ups and downs, but I wouldn't change a single footstep of our journey. I know our kids' compasses will always point north to Bayfield, and that makes me happy.

Fall

FALL IS MY SEASON. Bonfires, wool turtleneck sweaters, apple cider, hillsides blanketed in rich color, viscous golden afternoon light, the smell of pine from the sun hitting the golden needles on the ground, bread puddings, putting my garden to bed for the winter, beef stew, and roasted chicken . . . not to mention the blessed absence of black flies on the beach after the first frost. Fall is a gift that just keeps giving. It's all about preparing, preserving, and putting up firewood, pickles, beans, jams, tomato sauce, pesto, potatoes, and squash in the early part of fall, when summer is a recent memory and the first snowfall seems miles down the road. Moving toward days with a slower cadence, longer nights, wood fires in the stove, and those first, thrilling snowflakes inspires an ancient rhythm of taking stock and reflecting on the abundance of the harvest.

As I pickle and preserve my way through piles of the garden's largesse, I'm reminded to treasure these foods that are so freely given to my family. It's one thing to grab a tomato from the garden when the plants are going gangbusters and the supply seems endless, but it's an entirely other thing to open a jar of canned tomatoes in the middle of winter, when a decent tomato is nowhere to be found, and taste that sweetness long after the plant is gone. Fall is a pause between the riotous abundance of summer and the muffled repose of winter, a time to embrace and prepare for the coming stillness of a snow-covered world.

Julian Bay

OUR LAST BEACH DAY, at the end of September, was glorious. We made a spur-of-the-moment decision to hop in the *Karl* and head to Julian Bay on Stockton Island. The sun was too warm, the lake was too flat, and we were too excited to steal one last beach day to do anything but load up and go. It was the perfect early fall afternoon, full of capture the flag, walking the beach, and exploring the dunes.

On our way over, I had a feeling we would see a bear when we arrived at Julian Bay (Stockton has one of the highest concentration of black bears in the world). Unfortunately, we were a little late to watch him saunter down the beach, but he left his footprints behind.

Julian Bay is one of my favorite anchorages—it's open to the big lake, the sand "sings" when I walk on it, and the tombolo is an amazing contrast to the vast lake. It's the spot where I jumped off our sailboat, *Isle of Skye*, for the first time (with a life jacket on, of course), the backdrop for our famous Christmas card when Ted mooned the kids to get them to smile (he wasn't in the shot), where a fellow camper mistook Guinness, our Newfoundland, for a bear, where Meghan got up on water skis for the first time, and where I realized our lives had to be played out against the islands, lake, and hills of the Bayfield peninsula.

continued on next page

Stockton is a large island, over ten thousand acres, with three beaches (Julian, Presque Isle, and Quarry Bay), a tombolo (or sand bridge), and patches of wild huckleberries, thimbleberries, and cranberries. There was a Native American settlement here over a thousand years ago, a brownstone quarry in the 1800s, and in the recent past, fishing and hunting camps. Julian Nelson, a local fisherman and the namesake of Julian Bay, spent his childhood roaming the same beach and dunes my kids were playing on during our late September visit.

Julian and his family lived in a cabin on the northeast side of Julian Bay from 1918 to 1946, and Julian fished the waters of Lake Superior like his father did before him. The patch of blueberries that Julian and his siblings picked for their mother's pie is still there. A thrifty Norwegian, Andrea Jakobsen vetted the blueberry patches for the sweetest fruit because it required less sugar and directed her kids to gather buckets full for her blueberry pies. As I walked through the blueberry patch on my way back to the boat, I wondered how many other echoes of Julian's family remain on the island, and what echoes my family will leave behind.

Julian Bay hasn't changed much since Julian moved his cabin from Stockton to Rocky Island in 1946 and since the Apostle Islands were made into a national park in 1970; the beach, bay, and dunes have continued on, without human intervention. As we packed up and got ready to head back to Bayfield, I realized our echoes, like Julian's, are heard when we tell the story or share the photos of our last beach day of the year. And thanks to the National Park Service, the canvas of Julian Bay and its beach will remain unchanged and ready to hold the stories we have yet to write.

Roasted Butternut Squash and Goat Cheese Lasagna

I love everything about fall: golden light, shorter days, cooler weather, and the food, oh, the food. Provençal beef stew, roasted chickens, Indian curries, porchetta, bread puddings, lasagna…

I've embraced homemade pasta, even though it's more work than dried pasta. There is something meditative about standing at the counter, rolling and cutting the dough: forget yoga, I'll take my meditation with a side of lasagna. I'm also a firm believer in boiling pasta, and lasagna noodles are no exception. The no-boil method, at least with fresh pasta, doesn't taste as good. I can taste the raw flour, and I prefer the texture of noodles boiled for about a minute (if your sheets are thin, boil them for thirty seconds) prior to assembling the lasagna. An extra ten minutes yields a superior pan of lasagna, trust me.

SERVES 8

FOR THE FILLING

- 1 large butternut squash (about 3 pounds), cut in half lengthwise and seeded
- 10–12 medium cloves garlic, unpeeled
- 2 sprigs fresh thyme plus 2 teaspoons chopped thyme leaves
- 2 teaspoons extra-virgin olive oil
  Kosher salt
  Freshly ground black pepper
- 8 tablespoons butter, divided
- 1 large yellow onion, sliced
- ¼ cup all-purpose flour
- 3 cups whole milk
- 1½ cups fresh goat cheese
- 1 cup finely grated Pecorino Romano cheese
- 1 cup chopped cooked bacon, crumbled
- 1 cup freshly grated Parmesan cheese

FOR THE PASTA

- 2 cups all-purpose flour, plus more for rolling out
- 2 cups semolina flour (you can substitute all-purpose flour if you don't have semolina)
- 4 large eggs
- 3 tablespoons olive oil
- 1 teaspoon kosher salt
- ½ cup water, divided
- ¼ cup semolina flour or cornmeal, for dusting the sheet tray

continued on next page

Position a rack in the center of the oven and heat the oven to 425°F. Put the squash cut-side up on a large, heavy-duty rimmed baking sheet. Divide the garlic cloves and sprigs of thyme between the two halves and place in each cavity. Drizzle each half with 1 teaspoon of the oil and then season each with ¼ teaspoon salt and a few grinds of pepper. Roast until the squash is browned in spots and very tender when pierced with a skewer, 45 to 50 minutes. Remove from the oven and let cool completely.

Discard the thyme sprigs. Peel the garlic and put in a large bowl. Scoop the squash flesh from the skins and add it to the garlic. Mash with a fork until smooth. Season to taste with salt and pepper.

Melt 3 tablespoons of the butter in a sauté pan over medium heat. Add onions and 2 teaspoons chopped thyme, reduce heat to medium-low, and cook until golden brown and caramelized, about 45 minutes. Set aside.

Melt remaining 5 tablespoons butter in a 3-quart saucepan over medium heat. Add the flour and whisk until smooth and golden, about 2 minutes. Gradually whisk in the milk and cook, whisking occasionally, until thickened enough to coat the back of a spoon, about 15 minutes. Stir in the goat cheese, Pecorino, 1 teaspoon salt, and a few grinds of pepper. Season to taste with more salt and pepper.

In a large bowl, combine the cheese sauce, squash/garlic mixture, crumbled bacon, and caramelized onions. Stir to combine thoroughly and taste for seasoning. Set aside while making the pasta.

Combine both types of flour, eggs, olive oil, and salt in the bowl of a stand mixer. Turn the mixer on low and add 3 tablespoons of the water. Add more water, 1 tablespoon at a time, until the mixture comes together and forms a ball. Knead the dough on a lightly floured board to make sure it is well mixed. Set aside to rest for 30 minutes.

Generously flour your work area. Dust a sheet tray with semolina flour or cornmeal and set aside. Cut the dough into 6 pieces and cover with a towel (don't cover the pasta with kitchen towels if you use a scented fabric softener because the pasta will pick up the scent—use parchment instead). With your hands, flatten and shape one piece of dough into a ½-inch-thick rectangle. Dust it lightly with flour and pass it through the widest setting on the pasta machine. If the dough comes out oddly shaped, reform into a rectangle. Fold it in thirds, like a letter, and if necessary flatten to ½ inch thick. Pass it through the widest setting again, with the "seam" of the letter perpendicular to the rollers. Repeat this folding and rolling step five or six times, dusting the dough with flour if it becomes sticky. This is an important step in pasta making; you want to work the dough until it becomes silky and elastic.

Without folding the dough, pass it through the next narrowest setting on the pasta machine. Keep reducing the space between the rollers after each pass, lightly dusting the pasta with flour on both sides each time (I stop at setting number 6 on the KitchenAid pasta roller).

Generously dust both sides of the pasta sheet and lay it on the sheet tray. Immediately cut pasta sheet into lasagna noodles, about 13 inches long. Transfer strips to a drying rack for 1 hour; repeat with remaining dough.

Bring a 10-quart pot of well-salted water (it should taste like seawater) to a boil over high heat. Put a large bowl of ice water near the pot of boiling water. Line a rimmed baking sheet with sheets of parchment and have more parchment ready.

Put 3 or 4 noodles in the boiling water. Once the water returns to a boil, cook for 1 minute. With a large wire skimmer, carefully transfer noodles to the ice water to stop the cooking. Repeat with the remaining noodles. Drain the noodles and rinse under cold water. Spread them flat on the parchment-lined sheet tray (I layered them on top of each other and they didn't stick, but if you are concerned about sticking, layer the noodles between parchment.) Set aside until you're ready to assemble the lasagna.

Preheat oven to 350°F. Spread ½ cup of the cheese/squash sauce over the bottom of a 9x13-inch baking dish. Cover the sauce with a slightly overlapping layer of cooked noodles, cutting them as needed to fill any gaps. Spread 1 cup of the cheese/squash mixture evenly over the noodles and sprinkle with the Parmesan. Add another layer of noodles and repeat the layers as instructed above to make a total of 4 squash layers and 5 pasta layers. Spread the remaining cheese/squash sauce evenly over the top. Sprinkle with the remaining Parmesan cheese.

Cover the baking dish with foil and bake for 40 minutes. Remove the foil and bake until the top is browned and bubbly, 15 to 20 minutes. Cool for at least 10 minutes before serving.

MAKE-AHEAD INSTRUCTIONS

You can make the roasted squash mixture up to 1 day ahead of assembling the lasagna. You can assemble the lasagna up to 2 days ahead of baking it. Tightly wrap the baking dish in plastic wrap and refrigerate it. Let the lasagna come to room temperature before baking.

Maple-Glazed Duck

The night I made this duck for dinner started off with so much promise. Our good friends Julie and Charly were coming for dinner; our eldest son, Jack, was home from UW–Madison for the weekend; and four bottles of my latest delivery of mail-order wine (a lovely 2010 Chateau Hanteillan Haut Medoc) were perched on my counter. There was one fly in the ointment: an oven with a mind of its own that shut off halfway through the cooking process.

In spite of the oven debacle, that duck made a fine dinner on a crisp fall evening. The wine was delicious, the company was engaging, and the pieces of duck that were fully cooked were crispy skinned, tender, and infused with sweet maple and Dijon.

SERVES 4

FOR THE DUCK

1 (4- to 5-pound) roasting duck
  Kosher salt
1 yellow onion, peeled and roughly chopped
1 clementine, quartered
1 orange, quartered
3 sprigs thyme
3 sprigs of fresh rosemary
  Freshly ground black pepper

FOR THE GLAZE

½ cup maple syrup
¼ cup honey
¼ cup sherry vinegar
¼ cup port wine
¼ cup fresh orange juice
¼ cup Dijon mustard
1 tablespoon orange zest
2 teaspoons minced fresh thyme
2 teaspoons minced fresh rosemary
2 garlic cloves, minced

24 hours before roasting, place duck on a wire rack over a sheet tray and poke holes in the skin with a skewer or cut a crosshatch pattern all over the skin with a knife. Pat dry, season with kosher salt, and place duck in the refrigerator, uncovered, to allow skin to dry (this makes the skin get nice and crispy when it's in the oven).

Preheat oven to 375°F and remove duck from the refrigerator. Fill cavity with onion, clementine, orange, thyme, and rosemary. Tie legs together with twine and tuck wings behind back. Place duck on a rack in a heavy roasting pan, season with freshly ground pepper, and roast for 30 minutes.

While the duck is roasting, combine all of the glaze ingredients in a heavy-bottomed saucepan and cook over medium heat until combined. Begin to brush the duck with glaze after the duck has been in the oven for 30 minutes, and continue to baste every 15 minutes until the internal temperature reaches 155°F (about another 45 minutes). Raise the oven temperature to 425°F and cook until skin is crispy, about 10 minutes longer. Remove from oven and allow duck to rest for about 10 minutes.

Baked Sweet Potatoes with Cilantro Lime Butter

Fall announces itself in all sorts of ways in Bayfield: frosty mornings, late-afternoon sunsets, and geese winging their way south. But it's the deep oranges of fall that I love the most: pumpkins, squash, and sweet potatoes. The sweet potato's combination of earthy and slightly sweet flavors makes it a frequent player in my kitchen, and this recipe, with its bright green/citrusy butter, is a bridge between our technicolor summers and our more muted falls. I came up with this recipe when I owned a restaurant and needed an interesting potato recipe that would travel well, appeal to all sorts of eaters, and look pretty. And these sweet potatoes meet all three objectives beautifully: the bright green compound butter (or coconut oil if you want to make it vegan) against the deep orange of the sweet potato looks good enough to eat!

SERVES 6

6 sweet potatoes, washed and pricked with holes
½ cup butter (or coconut oil), softened
½ cup chopped fresh cilantro
1 garlic clove, minced
1 shallot, minced
1 teaspoon kosher salt
½ teaspoon cracked black pepper
½ teaspoon lime zest

Preheat oven to 400°F. Place the sweet potatoes on the middle rack and bake until soft, about 45 minutes. While the sweet potatoes are cooking, mix the remaining ingredients together and set aside.

When the potatoes are done, cut them in half and place some cilantro lime butter inside each potato. Put the potatoes back in the oven for a few minutes until the butter is melted, and then serve immediately.

Rituals of Fall

WHEN TED ASKED ME IF I WANTED TO GO FOR A RIDE on an early September afternoon, I knew it meant a drive down Echo Valley Road scouting for a tree to dispatch into firewood for the winter. Living in Bayfield has taught me the importance of moving with the cadence of the natural world, and harvesting—whether it's firewood from the forest, vegetables from the garden, or apples from the orchard—is a cherished ritual of autumn here in the north. It is work that's good for the spirit, preserving the bounty of summer for the snow-blanketed days ahead.

En route to our firewood safari, untended apple trees along the road caught my eye—the last witnesses to homesteads long since abandoned. I wondered about the stories that unfolded in those overgrown fields and under the fruit-laden trees that are remnants of families who chose to settle in this beautiful place. Bayfield, by virtue of its location on the peninsula, has a microclimate that's particularly well-suited for agriculture. Jesuits planted cherry trees on Madeline Island in the eighteenth century; lighthouse keeper Roswell Pendergast started a nursery on Michigan Island in 1870 that supplied apple, cherry, plum, peach, and pear trees to farmers in the region; and William Knight planted the first commercial apple and cherry orchard here in 1905. The apple trees I saw on the road and the orchards operating today are testaments to men and women who understood the intricate relationship between stewardship and a bountiful harvest.

Ellen Kwiatkoski and Eric Carlson, owners of Blue Vista Farm, view themselves as caretakers of a remarkable farm filled with raspberries, blueberries, and 1,500 apple trees. They practice the land ethic used by many of the farmers who continue to work the land around Bayfield; for them, true sustainability means maintaining the delicate balance between the harvest and the subsequent restoration of the land, trees, soil, and plants. At its heart, stewardship means understanding that we humans are transitory and that what we plant, nurture, and preserve reflects what we value.

When we live in concert with the earth and its rhythms, life becomes more predictable. Winter follows autumn, geese move from north to south and back again every year, trees sprout, grow, and die in one patch of soil in the forest, the sun rises and sets on the horizon every single day, and the harvest comes in after a season of expansion and growth. Harvest is a time to suspend the busy and chaotic business of living and offer thanks for the sheer abundance we receive. And to remember that while the harvest is freely given, the essence of its generosity is tied to our ability and desire to return the favor—in all of our actions and decisions.

Is a yard full of freshly split firewood or a pantry full of preserved beans, tomatoes, and apples enough to show my appreciation for the natural world? It's a step in the right direction, that's for sure. The act of gathering firewood, apples, or tomatoes goes hand in hand with restoration. When I prepare food that's grown with integrity, fill my woodstove with logs from the forests near my home, or spend time around a table heavy with the largesse of local gardens and orchards, I'm participating in the age-old ritual of honoring the harvest and celebrating the beautiful place I call home.

Pancetta and Pear Tartlets

These little tartlets are full of flavor, beautiful to behold, and easy to pull together. You can substitute apples or other pear varieties for the Asian pears I use—the key is just a little sweet fruit to play off the Gorgonzola and pancetta. I drizzle honey on the top of the tartlets to add a cohesive, glazed texture to the melted Gorgonzola.

MAKES SIX 4½-INCH TARTLETS

2 tablespoons butter, room temperature
1 package (20 ounces) puff pastry sheets thawed (I use Pepperidge Farms)
½ cup freshly shredded Parmesan cheese
1 Asian pear, thinly sliced
½ cup crumbled Gorgonzola cheese
¼ pound pancetta, diced
½ red onion, thinly sliced
3 teaspoons honey
   Maldon salt and cracked black pepper to taste

Preheat oven to 400°F and butter six tartlet pans well. Unfold a sheet of puff pastry on a lightly floured surface and roll out until it's about ¼-inch thick. Cut the pastry into individual rounds large enough to fit into your tartlet pans (mine are about 4½ inches in diameter) and place in the buttered pans.

Divide and sprinkle the Parmesan among the tartlet pans. Divide sliced pears, Gorgonzola, pancetta, and onions among the pans; drizzle each with honey and season with salt and pepper. Bake until golden brown and puffed, about 15 minutes. Remove from the pans and either serve immediately or let cool to room temperature.

Savory Gorgonzola Cheesecake

When I was in the throes of developing a menu for Good Thyme, my restaurant, in 2008, I really wanted to include a savory cheesecake. There's something about Gorgonzola that's so well suited to the crisp, cool days of fall. Its pungent, earthy flavors and creamy texture evoke wood smoke and the smell of fallen leaves in the sunlight. My partner, Renee, and I went round and round trying to winnow out the best appetizers for opening day, and this cheesecake lost out to a relish tray and a Reuben dip. But even though it didn't make the cut at the restaurant, it's a star in my kitchen.

SERVES 10 TO 12 AS AN APPETIZER

FOR THE CRUST

1	cup fresh bread crumbs (homemade or store-bought)
½	cup butter, melted
½	cup toasted and chopped pecans
⅓	cup freshly grated Parmesan cheese
1½	teaspoons all-purpose flour
½	teaspoon cayenne

FOR THE FILLING

12	ounces good-quality Gorgonzola cheese, at room temperature
12	ounces cream cheese, at room temperature
⅓	cup freshly shredded Parmesan cheese
1	tablespoon all-purpose flour
½	teaspoon minced mixed fresh herbs (such as rosemary, thyme, oregano, basil)
3	eggs
½	pear, peeled and thinly sliced
½	red onion, thinly sliced
½	teaspoon kosher salt
¼	teaspoon cracked black pepper

Blend all crust ingredients in a food processor until crumbly. Butter or spray with cooking spray the inside of an 8-inch springform pan and press the crust into the bottom and up the sides. Chill for 10 minutes.

Preheat the oven to 375°F. In a large bowl, using an electric mixer or a stand mixer, blend the Gorgonzola, cream cheese, Parmesan, flour, and herbs until well combined. Add the eggs, one at a time, beating well after each. Season with salt and pepper.

Place half of the pear and onion slices on the crust and then top with half of the cheesecake mixture. Place the remaining pears and red onion on top of the cheesecake mixture and top with remaining cheesecake mixture. Bake for 1 hour and 15 minutes. Turn the oven off, crack the door open, and let the cheesecake sit in the oven for another hour. Place the cheesecake in its springform pan in the refrigerator for 8 hours or overnight and then remove from pan. Serve with pear flatbread.

Dried Pear Flatbread

I made these crispy, savory flatbread crackers for the first time the night I met Lindsay Buckingham, of Fleetwood Mac fame, at Big Top Chautauqua. I had volunteered to make some appetizers for a "meet and greet" event after Buckingham's show (which was extraordinary), and I wanted to serve something more special than plain crackers with the Gorgonzola cheesecake. I don't know if Lindsay tried them, but they are definitely worthy of rock stars as well as civilians!

SERVES 10 TO 12

1	teaspoon instant yeast (I use SAF Red Instant Yeast)
1	cup warm water
1	teaspoon kosher salt
½	cup chopped dried pears
¼	cup chopped dried cranberries
¼	cup toasted and chopped pecans
2	tablespoons extra-virgin olive oil
1	teaspoon minced fresh rosemary
2½	cups bread flour

In a medium bowl, add the yeast to the water and salt and let sit for a few minutes. Add the pears, cranberries, pecans, olive oil, and rosemary and stir to blend. Stir in the flour and then knead for 1 minute. Cover the bowl with plastic wrap and let rest for 30 minutes.

Preheat the oven to 450°F and oil a baking sheet. Divide the dough into 4 pieces. Roll each piece ¼ to ½ inch thick on the baking sheet. Bake for 7 minutes. The flatbreads can be any shape that fits your pan. Break into cracker-sized pieces before serving.

Caramelized Apple Bread Pudding with Rum Caramel Sauce

Bread pudding is a brilliant use of stale bread, and when you add caramelized apples and a rum caramel sauce, it soars past ordinary brilliant and heads into quantum brilliance. We're not a dessert family (which could have something to do with the fact that we rarely finish dinner before nine), but one autumn night the stars aligned: we sat down to eat dinner at seven, there were two stale baguettes sitting on top of the fridge, and I had just picked up some apples from Blue Vista Farm. The pudding was a huge hit—and it was definitely worth eating dinner early so we could have dessert.

Caramelizing the apples until they are a deep golden color really makes a difference, so don't skip this step. It concentrates the apple flavors and helps them hold their own amid the custard-soaked bread cubes. This is terrific served with vanilla ice cream.

SERVES 10

FOR THE BREAD PUDDING

- 5 large tart apples (such as Jonagold or Honeycrisp)
- 3 tablespoons butter, plus more for greasing pan
- ½ cup plus 3 tablespoons dark brown sugar, divided
- 4 large eggs
- ½ cup maple syrup
- ½ teaspoon salt
- ½ teaspoon freshly grated nutmeg
- ¼ teaspoon cinnamon
- 2½ cups half and half
- 1 cup whole milk
- 1 teaspoon vanilla extract
- 8 cups stale bread cut into 1-inch cubes (reserve 1 cup for the topping)
- ½ cup chopped pecans

FOR THE CINNAMON-SUGAR TOPPING

- 1 tablespoon sugar
- ¼ teaspoon cinnamon
- 2 tablespoons butter, melted

FOR THE RUM CARAMEL SAUCE

- 6 tablespoons butter
- ½ cup cream
- 1 cup light brown sugar
- 3 tablespoons spiced rum

Preheat oven to 350°F and butter a 9x13-inch pan. Peel the apples and cut into 1-inch chunks. Melt butter in a 12-inch skillet over medium-high heat. Add 3 tablespoons brown sugar and stir until the mixture bubbles, then toss in the apples to coat them. Let the apples sit undisturbed, in a single layer if your pan is large enough, for a few minutes to sear the exterior, and then flip them over and let them sit another minute. Repeat this process until the apples are caramelized and tender, about 10 minutes. Remove the apples and juices from the pan and set aside.

In a large bowl, whisk together the eggs, remaining ½ cup brown sugar, maple syrup, salt, nutmeg, and cinnamon to combine. Add the half and half, milk, and vanilla and combine thoroughly.

Place 7 cups of the bread cubes in the large mixing bowl and toss to coat with the maple syrup/milk mixture. Let sit for about 45 minutes, tossing a few more times, and then place the bread cubes in the buttered baking dish. Place the caramelized apples, their reserved juices, and chopped pecans over the bread. Scatter the remaining cup of bread cubes over the apples and press them to partially submerge in the custard.

In a small bowl, combine 1 tablespoon sugar with ¼ teaspoon cinnamon. Brush the exposed bread cubes with the melted butter and sprinkle evenly with the cinnamon sugar.

Bake until the bread pudding is golden and a knife inserted into the middle comes out clean, about 45 minutes. Remove the pudding from the oven and let cool for at least 30 minutes.

While pudding is cooling, combine butter, cream, brown sugar and rum in a saucepan, bring to a boil, and simmer until slightly thickened, 2 to 3 minutes. Pour sauce over bread pudding and serve.

Pickled Apples

Once the apple harvest begins in Bayfield, it's all apples, all the time. A friend once asked me if it's possible to pickle apples and, having pickled grapes before, I thought, why not? I can't get over how many good things have resulted from that simple sentiment "why not?"—dogs, restaurants, boats, bottles of wine, running a 5K, and pickled apples are all great examples of throwing caution to the wind and adding some spice, sugar, and vinegar to our lives.

MAKES FOUR 1-QUART JARS

4	cups water
2	cups apple cider vinegar
1½	cups maple syrup
2	teaspoons kosher salt
3-inch piece of fresh ginger, thinly sliced	
1	small red onion, peeled and thinly sliced
1	star anise, broken into pieces
½	cinnamon stick, broken into pieces
¾	teaspoon mixed peppercorns
10	sweet-tart apples (Honeycrisp or Jonafree)
4	three-inch pieces of lemon rind
4	three- to four-inch sprigs of fresh rosemary

Clean and sterilize four 1-quart mason jars with lids.

In a large saucepan over medium-high heat, combine water, cider vinegar, maple syrup, salt, ginger, red onion, star anise, cinnamon stick, and peppercorns and bring to a boil. Lower the heat and simmer for 10 minutes.

Peel and core the apples and cut into rings or wedges. Divide the apple pieces, lemon rind, and rosemary sprigs among the jars. Carefully ladle the hot liquid over them (try to get a little cinnamon stick and star anise in each jar). Set aside for 15 minutes. Screw on the lids. Refrigerate for up to 3 months.

Note: Home canning carries food safety risks. For complete canning instructions, consult the University of Wisconsin Extension's many publications on home canning and preserving (http://fyi.uwex.edu/safepreserving) or the National Center for Home Food Preservation's resources (http://nchfp.uga.edu).

Hadley's Beach
Birthday

THE FIRST THING I NOTICED WHEN WE MOVED to Bayfield was that most cars had a dog riding shotgun. Dogs are held in high regard in northern Wisconsin, and for a die-hard dog lover like me, this was very good news.

Bayview Beach, about five miles from Bayfield, is our beach for morning walks with the pups, and we've met lots of other dog friends along the way, including Hadley, Maple, Luna, Madison, Tess, Zeus, and Rhodes. It's a de facto dog park for locals who like to get up early and watch the sun rise over the South Channel between Madeline and Long Islands. When my friend and equally enthusiastic dog lover Amber suggested a birthday party for her girl, Hadley, the boys and I were all in.

The morning of the party was shrouded in fog, but we forged ahead, and the dogs didn't seem to mind. We walked the beach before serving the treats, and by the time we were ready for the pumpkin ice cream, the dogs were covered in sand and soaking wet . . . not unlike the guests at a typical six-year-old boy's birthday party. We set the table, loaded the bowls with ice cream, and set them in front of the pups. Hadley, the birthday girl, decided to wait until the others were done eating; she likes to eat in front of an audience. It was the perfect foggy doggy birthday party.

Pumpkin Peanut Butter Dog Ice Cream

MAKES 6 CUPS OF ICE CREAM

1 tub (32 ounces) plain yogurt
1 cup canned pureed pumpkin
(*not* pumpkin pie filling)
½ cup all-natural peanut butter (make sure the peanut butter does not contain xylitol, as it's poisonous to dogs)

Combine yogurt, pumpkin, and peanut butter in a blender or food processor and blend until smooth. Pour mixture into a freezer-safe container or pour into ice cube trays for individual portions. Cover and freeze for 3 hours or until frozen solid. Scoop into a dish to serve.

Pressing
Apples into Cider

CIDER-PRESSING PARTIES ARE ONE OF THE HARBINGERS of fall in Bayfield, right up there with Applefest, the first fire in the woodstove, and the last boat ride on the lake. Fall in Bayfield is far from predictable, and a warm, sunny day in October is especially sweet because the late-afternoon sunsets and frozen mornings of winter are around the corner.

My friend Jill invited us over for an afternoon of apple pressing and cider collecting at her house down the road. It wasn't my first cider rodeo, so I knew what to expect: a lot of apples, a lot of elbow grease, and a few decent-sized jars of raw apple cider. The apple world has its own language (a peck is 10 pounds, and a bushel is 45 pounds), and making a couple of gallons of cider takes a couple pecks of apples. That's a lot of apples—and when you're picking them yourself, it seems like even more apples.

Meghan and her friend Caroline were my partners in pressing. While I took photos, they dropped the apples into the chute, cranked the handle to break the apples into pieces, and turned the press until the apples surrendered their juice into the glass jars. Between the wheelbarrows full of exhausted apple pulp, the cast-iron pan full of roasted garlic, and the jars of chestnut-colored fresh cider, it was a photographic wonderland.

The pressing went along quickly as we had plenty of helping hands available to wash apples, crank the press, and fill the jars. We discussed the provenance of the apples (wild picked or farm purchased), what variety of apple yields the best cider, and if cider should be canned to hold it well into the winter. As the sun began to dip behind the treetops and we were reminded that it was October, not August, I felt the blessing of a day spent outside among friends, bottling the last fruit of the harvest season. It was good to gather up the summer sun and rain to enjoy when it's snowing sideways.

Roasted Apple and Chipotle Butter

Apples lend themselves remarkably well to savory dishes. Serve this apple butter alongside a roasted chicken, stir a little into polenta, or smear it on a warm buttermilk biscuit. Its trifecta of flavors—sweet, smoky, and spicy—really livens up a meal.

MAKES ABOUT 3 CUPS OF APPLE BUTTER

5	tablespoons butter, divided
1	large shallot, chopped
½	cup Calvados or apple brandy
3	pounds Cortland or Jonafree apples (or your favorite tart apple), peels left on
2	cups apple cider, divided
½	cup brown sugar
1½	tablespoons freshly squeezed lemon juice
3–5	chipotle peppers in adobo, minced (quantity depending on your heat tolerance)
1	teaspoon cinnamon
¼	teaspoon nutmeg
¼	teaspoon kosher salt

In a medium skillet, heat 1 tablespoon butter over medium heat. Add the shallot to the pan, lower the heat, and sauté for about 10 minutes. Add the Calvados and set aside.

Preheat oven to 375°F. Cut the apples into eighths and place in a large roasting pan (do not peel or remove the seeds). Add 1 cup of the apple cider, the brown sugar, the remaining 4 tablespoons butter, and the lemon juice. Toss to combine and place in the oven until the apples are very soft and lightly browned, about 45 minutes. Remove the pan from the oven and pour the remaining 1 cup of cider over the top, stirring to remove any caramelized apple bits from the bottom of the pan.

Transfer the apples and liquid to a large bowl and mash with a potato masher (or fork) until it looks saucy. Run the mixture through a food mill to remove the seeds and skins. Add the reserved shallot mixture, minced chipotles, cinnamon, nutmeg, and salt. If the butter is too runny, transfer to a saucepan and cook over low heat on the stovetop, stirring occasionally, until it's the consistency you want. If you prefer a smoother texture, once the butter is cooled, you can blend it in a food processor or blender. Store in an airtight container in the refrigerator for up to a week.

Dutch Baby with Cider Syrup

My sister Bridget's first job was at Sytje's Pannekoeken Huis in Richfield, Minnesota, and the uniform was straight out of Holland (or someone's idea of Holland), complete with the long dress, pinafore, and little white hat. Given our Irish Catholic heritage, the word *pannekoeken* seemed downright exotic, until I learned it was just a fancy name for a baked fluffy pancake. Dutch baby has a whole new meaning when I think about Bridget and her server outfit, and I think of her every time I pull one of these babies out of the oven!

SERVES 4

FOR THE CIDER SYRUP

- 4 cups apple cider
- 2 tablespoons butter
- 1 tablespoon brown sugar
- 1 tablespoon vanilla
- ½ teaspoon cinnamon

FOR THE DUTCH BABY

- 3 eggs
- ¾ cup buttermilk
- ¾ cup flour
- 1 tablespoon vanilla
- 1½ teaspoons cinnamon, divided
- ¼ teaspoon kosher salt
- 4 tablespoons butter, divided
- 2 large apples, peeled and sliced
- 1 tablespoon brown sugar
- 4 ounces cream cheese, cut into ½-inch pieces

To make the syrup, combine cider, butter, brown sugar, vanilla, and cinnamon in a heavy-bottomed, shallow pan and simmer until thick and syrupy, about 1 to 1½ hours. This mixture can be made ahead of time and stored in the refrigerator; gently warm the syrup in a small saucepan prior to serving.

Preheat oven to 425°F. Whisk eggs, buttermilk, flour, vanilla, 1 teaspoon cinnamon, and salt in a large bowl until smooth; set batter aside.

Melt 2 tablespoons of butter in a cast-iron skillet and add the apples, brown sugar, and remaining ½ teaspoon cinnamon. Cook over medium heat, stirring often, until softened (about 5 minutes) and transfer to a plate.

Wipe out skillet and place in oven until very hot, about 10 minutes. Remove from oven and add remaining 2 tablespoons of butter and swirl to coat the bottom and sides. Add the apples to the center and pour the batter over them. Sprinkle the cream cheese pieces over the batter and return to oven. Bake until the pancake is puffed and golden brown, 12 to 15 minutes. Remove from oven and top with warm apple cider syrup.

Lost Creek Falls

A FRIEND SUGGESTED THAT WILL AND I EXPAND our photo safari grounds to a waterfall in the forest near Cornucopia. With a name like Lost Creek and the vague directions (*park near the cemetery, walk down a trail through the woods, look for an ATV trail, take a left into another pine forest, go up and down through multiple ravines, and the waterfall is down a steep embankment*), I figured it was a contender for "the most epic photo safari ever"—and until we attempted to photograph Potato Falls in February, it was.

Since that auspicious beginning, we've been back to Lost Creek Falls many times. There are two waterfalls on Lost Creek No. 1. The first cascades over moss-covered brownstone steps into Lost Creek and flows toward the second waterfall about a quarter-mile downstream. The second waterfall is stunning: water flows over a sandstone shelf about fifteen feet into a shallow pool and continues to wind its way toward the lake. I've sat behind that waterfall and peered through the curtain of water at my kids building cairns, taking pictures, and exploring the streambed and felt completely and utterly at home. The waterfalls, ravines, pines, rocks, and streams are familiar now, I recognize the trees and stumps that line the path, and I navigate by memory, not directions. That's the extraordinary part of finding home; it feels like I've been here all along.

Now that I wake up under pines every morning, it still feels good. Living in a town of four hundred people has its challenges, but as Terry Tempest Williams said, committing to a community isn't necessarily easy, "but it does mean you can live with patience, because you're not going to go away." The unexpected treasure I discovered when I committed myself to this patch of earth is that the trees, flowers, lake, waterfalls, and creeks are equally committed and "living with patience" beside me.

The blessing in finding home, beyond the contentment that accompanies setting down roots, is the ability to mark your life against the predictable and steadfast backdrop of the natural world. I've calibrated my inner compass to the huge white pine in my yard, to the basin of Lost Creek Falls, to Julian Bay on Stockton Island, to the Siskiwit River near Cornucopia, and to St. Peter's Dome in the Penokees. I spent my forty-fourth birthday walking down a path I've traveled many times before, through the pines to Lost Creek Falls and into the embrace of running water, cedars, sandstone, and birch trees. There is wild comfort in knowing Lost Creek Falls will be flowing long after I'm gone and that when my kids want to find the tether that will lead them back to me, it's as simple as a walk through the pines to flowing water among the cedars.

It's not complicated to commit to one place, but it is a radical concept in a world where travel, movement, and expansion are the norms. Our home is full of people who will become good friends, landscapes that will become way markers, the sound of waterfalls and wind in the pines that will become birthday songs, and seasons that will be marked by where the sun rises and sets on the horizon. In some small way, I'll leave my mark around Bayfield, and the most spectacular treasure of all is that my children and grandchildren will know exactly where to look.

Chicken Thighs with Asian Flair

Sadie's playing volleyball in Duluth, Meghan joined the swim team in Bayfield, and Charlie's developed a very busy social calendar in Washburn. Given the potential for a scheduling fiasco, quick and easy dinners are the name of the game. The criteria are simple: meals need to taste good and can't require much beyond a sheet tray and a preheated oven. This recipe fits the bill perfectly. Marinate the chicken overnight, add a rice cooker full of jasmine rice to the equation, and I am a picture of efficiency . . . kind of. There are still the issues of conflicting schedules, a lack of toilet paper, and the forty-two kinds of mustard in the fridge, but at least I can get dinner on the table before eight P.M.

SERVES 4 TO 6

½ cup olive oil
½ cup soy sauce
¼ cup apple cider vinegar
¼ cup palm sugar (you can substitute light brown sugar)
6 garlic cloves, chopped
1 jalapeño, seeded and chopped
3-inch piece of fresh ginger, peeled and minced
3 tablespoons fish sauce
3 tablespoons chili-garlic sauce
6 sprigs of thyme, de-stemmed and coarsely chopped
8 bone-in, skin-on chicken thighs

Combine olive oil, soy sauce, apple cider vinegar, sugar, garlic, jalapeño, ginger, fish sauce, chili-garlic sauce, and thyme. Whisk until the sugar is dissolved. Combine the chicken and marinade in a nonreactive bowl or resealable plastic bag, turn to coat chicken pieces well, and marinate for 12 hours or overnight.

Heat oven to 450°F and line a sheet tray with parchment. Remove the chicken from the marinade and place on tray. Roast until an instant-read thermometer registers 165°F, about 30 minutes. Serve immediately.

Chicken and Tomatillo Chili

Chili is a family favorite, and it makes an appearance at dinner a couple of times a month. What's not to love about a steaming bowl of meat in a spicy sauce topped with sour cream and cheese? I had a bunch of tomatillos on the counter, chicken thighs in the freezer, and my favorite Carmelina tomatoes on the shelf—it looked like chili was on the dinner docket. I always make a double batch so I can freeze the leftovers; having food in the freezer gives me a sense of security, like a dinner safety net.

SERVES 8 TO 10

2	tablespoons oil
2	red onions, chopped
3	red bell peppers, seeded and chopped
2	serrano peppers, seeded and minced
¼	cup cumin
¼	cup ancho chile powder
3	tablespoons Tajin Clásico seasoning
2	tablespoons oregano
2	tablespoons chili powder
1	tablespoon sugar
2	teaspoons kosher salt
12	boneless, skinless chicken thighs
36	tomatillos, halved
2	cans (28 ounces each) chopped tomatoes in puree
3	cans (15 ounces each) pinto beans (or any kind of bean you prefer)
½	cup chopped fresh cilantro, plus more for serving
	Sour cream and shredded cheddar cheese, for serving

Heat oil in a large sauté pan over medium-high heat and add onions. Sauté until onions are softened and golden brown, about 10 minutes. Add bell peppers, serrano peppers, cumin, ancho chile powder, Tajin, oregano, chili powder, sugar, and salt and sauté until the spices are fragrant, about 5 minutes.

Cut the chicken thighs into 1-inch pieces. In a medium stockpot or crockpot, combine chicken, sautéed vegetables, tomatillos, and canned tomatoes and their liquid. Cook in a slow cooker on low for 6 to 8 hours or simmer, uncovered, on the stovetop for 45 minutes. Add the beans and cilantro and cook for an additional 30 minutes. Serve immediately with sour cream, shredded cheese, and more fresh cilantro.

Carrot Cake with Ginger Mascarpone Frosting

I thought having five kids under ten made life busy, but having a houseful of teenagers is a whole different busy beast. Between forensics practice, soccer games, middle school dances, and sleepovers, I've come to cherish the nights when we all eat together. This carrot cake is a great way to celebrate a family dinner, and it keeps the kids around the table for another ten minutes, bantering and laughing their way into the next day full of busyness.

MAKES I LAYER CAKE

FOR THE CAKE

2	cups light brown sugar
1	cup vegetable oil
⅓	cup butter, softened
3	extra-large eggs
1½	tablespoons vanilla extract
2	cups all-purpose flour
2	teaspoons ground cinnamon
1½	teaspoons kosher salt
1	teaspoon ground ginger
1	teaspoon baking soda
1	teaspoon baking powder
½	teaspoon cardamom
1	pound carrots, grated
½	cup chopped dried pears

FOR THE GINGER MASCARPONE FROSTING

3	cups powdered sugar
16	ounces mascarpone cheese, at room temperature
16	ounces cream cheese, at room temperature
3	tablespoons peeled and grated fresh ginger
2	tablespoons vanilla extract
⅛	teaspoon kosher salt

Preheat the oven to 350°F. Grease two 9-inch round cake pans and line the bottoms with parchment paper.

In the bowl of a stand mixer fitted with the paddle attachment, beat the brown sugar, oil, butter, and eggs on medium-high speed for 2 minutes. Add the vanilla and mix to combine. In a separate bowl, combine the flour, cinnamon, salt, ginger, baking soda, baking powder, and cardamom. Stir to combine and then add dry ingredients to the oil/egg mixture. Stir until just combined. Fold in the carrots and pears. Divide the batter between the two cake pans and bake until a toothpick inserted near the center comes out clean, about 45 minutes. Cool in the pans for 10 minutes and then turn onto a wire rack and cool completely.

While the cakes are cooling, prepare the frosting. In the bowl of a stand mixer fitted with a paddle attachment, combine powdered sugar, mascarpone, cream cheese, ginger, vanilla, and salt; beat until smooth and fluffy. Spread the frosting on one cake layer; top with the second layer and cover completely with frosting. Serve immediately or cover and place in the refrigerator.

To Farm Well

I SPENT A FALL AFTERNOON WITH BETH DOOLEY, a cookbook author and friend from Minneapolis, who was leading a Bayfield farm tour during the height of harvest season. We visited North Wind Organic Farm, Blue Vista Farm, and Flying Snakes Farm—three farms operated by men and women who care deeply about their land and the harvest they produce.

Terroir, the concept that says our food reflects the place where it was grown or raised, has its roots in the French word *terre*, meaning land. French winemakers observed differences in wines from different regions or vineyards and developed the concept of terroir as a way to describe the unique aspects of a place that influence and shape the wine made from it. At its heart, terroir represents the interplay between nature and farmer. The uniqueness of Bayfield's natural environment is reflected in the food grown here, but our unique cultural methods, habits, and customs also play a part in those bushels of apples or pails of berries.

All the orchards and fruit farms on the Bayfield peninsula are family owned and operated (some for multiple generations), and the farmers' knowledge of the terroir here has a tremendous impact on the quality of the food they bring to market. There is a saying that a "vineyard's best fertilizer is the owner's footsteps," and that idea extends to any patch of earth that's been cultivated to produce the food we eat. Since farmers hold the knowledge of the soil, weather, water, vegetation, and animals unique to their farms, they are able to work with, not against, the forces of nature.

My son Charlie spent a summer working at Blue Vista Farm, and on his first day, founder Eric Carlson walked him through the fields and described the history and unique environment of the farm. From the beneficial insects in the fields to the crab-apple trees he planted as a windbreak for the berry bushes and apple trees, Eric has an intimate knowledge of his land. Like all good farmers, he's invested time and energy to understand the ecosystem that grows his crops.

That commitment was shared by all three farmers we visited on that late summer afternoon. Wendell Berry, author of *Bringing It to the Table: Writings on Farming and Food,* eloquently describes the intricate balance between the land and farmer: "Agriculture must mediate between nature and the human community, with ties and obligations in both directions. To farm well requires an elaborate courtesy toward all creatures, animate and inanimate." And farming well matters—it's the cornerstone of a healthy community.

Braised Cabbage with Quince, Apple, and Cranberries

Ted walked into the kitchen just as I remarked to myself (out loud) about the beautiful symmetry of the head of cabbage I had just cut in half. Thankfully, he's used to my mutterings in an empty room, but my cabbage love was a new one. If I remember correctly, I think Ted said something to the effect of, "I've never heard anyone call cabbage beautiful." Well, it is beautiful, and it tastes amazing after an hour spent ruminating with some fruit, apple cider, and vinegar.

SERVES 8

2	tablespoons butter
1	medium red onion, chopped
1½	heads of red cabbage, sliced into ribbons and rough chopped
2	teaspoons kosher salt
½	cup maple syrup
½	cup apple cider
¼	cup apple essence (see recipe on page 175)
6	tablespoons apple cider vinegar
2	cups whole fresh cranberries
1	tart apple, peeled and rough chopped
1	quince, peeled and rough chopped (if you can't find quince, substitute a tart apple)

Heat a large Dutch oven over medium heat. Add butter and onion and cook, covered, for about 10 minutes. Uncover and cook for 5 minutes longer, stirring occasionally.

Add cabbage and salt and cook until cabbage is wilted, 5 to 7 minutes. Add maple syrup, apple cider, apple essence, and cider vinegar to the Dutch oven and simmer uncovered, stirring occasionally, for 20 minutes. Add cranberries, apple, and quince and stir to combine. Cover and cook until the cabbage is softened, about 20 minutes longer. Serve immediately.

Venison Bacheofe

When our friend Charly offered me two venison roasts, I knew exactly what to make for dinner. Earlier in the week, Ted had asked me if I could find a recipe for the Alsatian casserole made at the Black Forest in Minneapolis. While I had no luck tracking down the Black Forest version, I found an intriguing recipe for an Alsatian bacheofe—a slow-cooked stew topped with a dough rope that creates the perfect braising environment. The dough seals every ounce of flavorful braising liquid in the pot, where it works its magic on the meat and vegetables.

When I broke the seal, I kind of felt like Geraldo Rivera when he opened Al Capone's vault, except my "vault" was full of tender meat, potatoes, and carrots. I served my venison bacheofe with braised red cabbage, a perfect contrast to the richness of the meat. This does require a little forethought (the meat and vegetables marinate overnight), but like all braises, it was about as easy as it gets and makes a perfect meal when the sun sets at four-thirty and the forest is blanketed in amber and russet hues. Here's to fall and all the hearty braises that make it my favorite season.

SERVES 8 TO 10

4 pounds venison chuck or shoulder roast, cut into 1½-inch pieces
   Kosher salt and freshly ground black pepper
4 cups dry white wine, such as Alsatian Riesling
6 sprigs fresh thyme
6 garlic cloves, minced
2 bay leaves
2 tablespoons chopped rosemary
8 tablespoons butter, divided
4 medium carrots, peeled and sliced
4 parsnips, peeled and sliced
3 medium yellow onions, chopped
1 cup fresh whole cranberries
¼ cup duck fat (available at good meat markets or online)
3 pounds Yukon Gold potatoes, sliced
1 pound bacon, uncooked
1 cup flour
5 tablespoons water

Place venison in a bowl and season all over with salt and pepper. Combine wine, thyme sprigs, garlic, bay leaves, and rosemary in a bowl and mix well. Pour over the venison, cover, and refrigerate for up to 24 hours.

Preheat oven to 350°F. Remove the venison from the marinade and set the marinade aside. Season the venison with salt. Heat a large sauté pan over medium-high heat, melt 2 tablespoons of butter, and brown one-quarter of the meat mixture evenly on all sides. Set browned meat aside. Repeat, adding 2 tablespoons of butter each time, until all the meat has been browned.

Combine carrots, parsnips, onions, and cranberries in a bowl and set aside. Rub the sides and bottom of a large cast-iron Dutch oven with duck fat. Layer potatoes, then venison, and then vegetables in the pot, seasoning each layer with salt and pepper, ending with a layer of potatoes. You will end up with three layers of venison and vegetables, with the fourth layer of potatoes. Pour the remaining marinade into the Dutch oven and arrange the bacon over the top layer of potatoes.

Mix the flour and water in a bowl, knead briefly to combine, and roll into a rope long enough to encircle the rim of your Dutch oven. Firmly press the rope of dough on the rim of your Dutch oven and cover with the lid. Bake for 4 hours. Remove from the oven and, using a knife, break the dough seal and remove the lid.

Duck Fat Chicken with Roasted Vegetables

Duck fat is magic. Seriously. What it does to vegetables and chicken is lovely, as in very-crispy-skin lovely. Given the popularity of the paleo and high-quality-fat-is-good-for-you diets, duck fat is readily available these days. A quick internet search turns up plenty of options, and a good meat market or grocery store might carry it as well.

SERVES 6

1   whole chicken (preferably organic)
⅓   cup duck fat
½   cup chopped fresh herbs (basil, thyme, rosemary, oregano—combination of any or all), divided
1   tablespoon minced shallot
1   clove garlic, minced
1   teaspoon kosher salt, plus more to taste
½   teaspoon cracked black pepper, plus more to taste
3   carrots, peeled and sliced lengthwise
2   pounds of red potatoes, quartered
1   large onion, sliced
2   tablespoons olive oil

Preheat oven to 400°F and line a sheet tray with parchment. Spatchcock the chicken (remove the backbone and then flatten the chicken by pressing on the breastbone). Loosen the skin over the breasts, thighs, and legs. Mix the duck fat, ¼ cup of the chopped herbs, shallot, garlic, 1 teaspoon salt, and ½ teaspoon pepper in a small bowl and then place the mixture under the skin of the chicken.

Combine carrots, potatoes, and onions in a large bowl. Add olive oil and remaining ¼ cup fresh herbs. Mix to coat the vegetables with the oil; season with salt and pepper.

Place the chicken on a sheet tray and arrange the vegetables around the chicken. Roast until an instant-read thermometer says 165°F when inserted in the thickest part of the thigh, about 1 hour, stirring the vegetables about halfway through to ensure they are evenly coated with the duck fat. Transfer the chicken and vegetables to a platter and let stand for 10 minutes before carving.

Herring Harvest
at Bodin Fisheries

BAYFIELD IS A WORKING harbor town, complete with three retail fish shops with fresh and smoked fish, a fish-processing plant, and fishing tugs in the harbor. The tugs go out in the morning to check the gill nets they've set around the islands and return hours later, loaded with fish that ends up on our tables and in restaurants and grocery stores around the region and state. It feels timeless, seeing a tug headed for home, seagulls billowing around the stern and picking up the scraps from the day's catch. It could just as easily be 1940 or 2017,

and that's a remarkable thing—that our historical tethers are intact in a world that is changing so fast.

The Bodins have fished the waters around Bayfield for five generations. Nils Bodin emigrated from Sweden in the late 1800s and settled in Ashland, Wisconsin, where he was a carpenter and fisherman. Over the past hundred years, the Bodins have fished for whitefish, trout, and herring in Lake Superior and grown into the largest wholesale fish processor in the area.

They process herring, a small whitefish also called cisco or bluefin, from Lake Superior waters ranging from the North Shore of Minnesota to the Chequamegon Bay in Wisconsin. Herring live in the deep, colder waters but move toward the shallower and warmer waters near shore during spawning season in the fall. The herring season runs from mid-October to the end of November, and as Jeff Bodin, fourth-generation fisherman, says, "It's nonstop processing until the harvest is over." After visiting the processing plant in mid-November, I can attest to the nonstop pace: the line is full of fish, roe, and the constant motion of hands moving and slicing the herring as they make their way into the plastic crates at the end.

Very little is wasted during processing: the herring goes to a plant in Iowa, where it's used for gefilte (a kosher fish loaf), the caviar is shipped to Scandinavia and all over the United States, and the waste goes to a plant in Algoma, Wisconsin, where it's processed into fertilizer. It's impressive that fish from Lake Superior ends up halfway across the world—as far away as Sweden, New York, and Florida. And it all starts near the docks at Bodin Fisheries.

Janel's Pickled Herring

My friend Janel used to own a restaurant on Madeline Island, and she and her husband, Richie, have been pickling herring for years. Their jars of silver herring floating in brine have reached almost iconic status—they're that good. I'm lucky to live in a place where fresh herring is available. And while pickling herring takes some time, every fishy, vinegary bite is worth it. Given that herring season hits its peak in November and this recipe makes a lot of pickled herring, you'll have plenty of hostess and holiday gifts at the ready in your fridge! Serve on buttered pumpernickel or with sliced hard-boiled egg and mayonnaise on toasted rye bread.

MAKES ABOUT 7 QUARTS OF PICKLED HERRING

5	pounds herring fillets
4	cups water
1	cup pickling salt
4–5	cups white vinegar (enough to cover the fish)
6	cups white vinegar, plus more to cover fish in bowl
4¼	cups sugar
15	whole cloves
12	bay leaves
1	tablespoon whole allspice
2	tablespoons mustard seeds
1½	tablespoons whole black peppercorns
2	white or yellow onions, sliced
1	lemon, sliced

Skin fish and cut into bite-sized pieces. Place the fish, water, and pickling salt in a glass or other nonreactive container, cover, and chill for 48 hours. Drain and rinse fish and return it to the rinsed nonreactive container. Cover the fish with white vinegar and chill for 24 hours.

Combine 6 cups white vinegar, sugar, cloves, bay leaves, allspice, mustard seeds, and peppercorns in a saucepan and bring to a boil over medium-high heat. Remove from heat and let cool.

Remove fish from white vinegar and rinse thoroughly. Place alternating layers of fish, onions, and lemon slices in a glass quart jar and pour brine over the top. Repeat with remaining ingredients. Cover and store jars in refrigerator for 5 days; shake daily. Will keep in the refrigerator for 1 month.

Grilled Lake Trout

Grilling a whole fish is the final frontier of mastering the grill. For the anglers among us, there is almost no greater culinary pleasure than a fresh, perfectly grilled fish landed by the griller him- or herself.

SERVES 6 TO 8

1   whole lake trout, cleaned,
    with skin left on
3   garlic cloves, finely chopped
2   tablespoons roughly chopped fresh
    rosemary, plus a handful of sprigs
2   tablespoons roughly chopped fresh
    thyme, plus a handful of sprigs
2   tablespoons roughly chopped oregano,
    plus a handful of sprigs
2   tablespoons roughly chopped chives,
    plus a handful of sprigs
    Salt and freshly ground pepper to taste
½   cup white wine
½   cup olive oil
2   lemons, sliced
1   red onion, sliced
¼   cup mayonnaise, plus more if needed

With a very sharp knife, score the skin on both sides of the fish on the diagonal at 1-inch intervals. Place trout in a shallow dish.

In a small bowl, combine the garlic and chopped herbs. Rub the herb-garlic paste all over the outside and inside of the fish and season with salt and pepper. Pour the white wine and olive oil over the fish, turn to coat, and let stand at room temperature for 30 minutes.

Prepare a charcoal or gas grill for direct grilling over medium-high heat. Brush and oil the grill grate and a fish-grilling basket.

Remove the fish from the marinade; discard the marinade and pat the fish dry. Stuff the fish cavities with the lemons, onion slices, and herb sprigs. Rub about ¼ cup (more or less depending on the size of your fish) mayonnaise on the skin of the fish (this will prevent the fish from sticking to the grill and does not leave a taste after it's cooked).

Place the fish in the basket and place on the grill directly over medium-high heat. Try to keep the grill temperature at 350–375°F. Grill, turning once, until skin is nicely charred and flesh is flaky and opaque down to the bone, 6 to 15 minutes (depending on the size of the fish). The fish is done when the internal temperature is 130°F. Let the fish rest for 5 minutes and then serve.

Foster Falls in the Fall

It has always been a happy thought to me that the creek runs on all night, new every minute, whether I wish it or know it or care, as a closed book on a shelf continues to whisper to itself its own inexhaustible tale. So many things have been shown me on these banks, so much light has illumined me by reflection here where the water comes down, that I can hardly believe that this grace never flags, that the pouring from ever-renewable sources is endless, impartial, and free.

—ANNIE DILLARD, *PILGRIM AT TINKER CREEK*

FOSTER FALLS CAME NEAR THE END of our fall magical mystery tour of the waterfalls in northwestern Wisconsin, and it was a good one. Again, I had a general idea of where to go, but a "general idea" is in no way related to good, solid directions. When we stopped at the O'Doveros' for some beef, I asked Wendy for directions to Wren Falls (our first destination), and she gave us the inside scoop on how to get there. Except

I didn't write anything down. Later I remembered everything up to "Turn left on Casey Sag Road and look for a fork in the road."

It turns out there are *two* forks in the road; we took the first one. Our cell phones were out of service range, but I figured the best way to find a waterfall was to find some water, and we did: the picturesque Potato River (without a waterfall in sight). As we walked back to the car, we noticed an ATV trail along the river, and Charlie ran ahead to scout out the situation. He came running back with good news: there was a trail (marked by a beer can on a branch) and a waterfall straight ahead. You've got to love good old Wisconsin way markers.

As we approached the falls, I realized we had taken the wrong turn at the fork; we were at Foster Falls, not Wren. It was a good wrong turn. Foster Falls is remarkable because you can walk up to the edge, sit on a flat piece of basalt, and feel the water and spray as they move down the cascade. Foster Falls is on the Potato River, a principal tributary in the Bad River Watershed, and is upstream from Potato River Falls. While it's lacking the serious wow factor of Potato River Falls, it's still impressive—twenty-five feet of tannin-stained, pristine, rushing water down a chute of basalt. The rocks soak up the sun and warm up nicely, making them a perfect spot for a picnic.

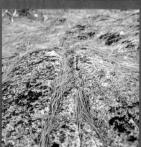

Apple Cider Farro with Gorgonzola

Farro is a hearty grain from Italy with a nutty earthiness that is well-suited to the fall flavors of Gorgonzola and apples. This salad is super easy to throw together and is a nice accompaniment to roasted duck or chicken. Be sure to use the semi-pearled variety—*semiperlato* in Italian; some of the bran has been removed, which allows for speedier cooking.

SERVES 4

3	cups apple cider
1	cup water
2	teaspoons kosher salt
1½	cups semi-pearled farro, uncooked
½	cup extra-virgin olive oil
¼	cup apple cider vinegar
1	tablespoon Dijon mustard
½	sweet-tart apple, cored and chopped
½	red onion, sliced
½	cup crumbled Gorgonzola cheese
2	tablespoons chopped fresh thyme
1	tablespoon chopped fresh rosemary
	Salt and pepper to taste

Combine apple cider, water, and salt in a saucepan and bring to a boil over medium-high heat. Add the farro and reduce to a simmer. Cook until the farro is al dente, about 30 minutes, and drain. Let cool.

In a small bowl, combine the olive oil, cider vinegar, and Dijon to make a vinaigrette. Place the cooked farro in a large salad bowl and add the vinaigrette. Toss to thoroughly combine. Add the apple, red onion, Gorgonzola, thyme, and rosemary and toss again. Taste for seasoning and add salt and pepper if necessary. Serve at room temperature.

Warm Potato Salad with Pancetta

I have a thing for pancetta—not just any old plastic-wrapped, sliced-too-thin pancetta, but the white-butcher-paper-wrapped fresh pancetta from Northern Waters Smokehaus in Duluth. Given my Irish heritage, I also have a thing for potatoes, and for the sole reason that it tastes good, I really like German potato salad. This version is "lick your plate clean" good, and it's equally good warm or room temperature, so it's just right for a picnic that requires a bit of a trek to reach the perfect spot.

SERVES 6

1	pound baby Yukon Gold potatoes
1	pound sweet potatoes, peeled and cut into cubes
6	tablespoons butter, divided
1	Vidalia onion, sliced
3–5	sprigs of lemon thyme (you can substitute regular thyme)
¼	pound pancetta, diced (I get mine at the Northern Waters Smokehaus)
3	tablespoons champagne vinegar
1	tablespoon stone-ground mustard
	Salt and coarsely ground pepper to taste
2	tablespoons chopped fresh chives

Bring a large saucepan of salted water to a boil. Add the Yukon Gold and sweet potatoes and cook over high heat until tender, about 10 minutes. Drain, shaking off any excess water.

Meanwhile, in a large skillet, melt 3 tablespoons of the butter over medium heat. Add the sliced onions and thyme sprigs and sauté until golden brown, about 10 minutes. Remove the onions and thyme, add the pancetta to the pan, and cook over medium heat, stirring frequently, until just beginning to brown, about 3 minutes. Add the remaining 3 tablespoons of butter and cook, stirring occasionally, until the pancetta is golden and the butter is just beginning to brown, about 2 minutes longer.

Whisk the vinegar and mustard into the pancetta mixture; season with salt and pepper. Add the potatoes and the chives and toss until evenly coated. Serve the potato salad warm or at room temperature.

Mrs. Pitts's Sugar Cookies

I was born in Steilacoom, Washington, and I have that beginning to thank for my love of cloudy days, wide expanses of water, ferries, and sugar cookies. We lived in an apartment above Mrs. Pitts, who sometimes gave me one of these cookies when we ran into her. According to my mom, I began to keep a sharp lookout for Mrs. Pitts and her cookies every time we left our apartment. Thankfully, she gave my mom the recipe before we moved back to Minnesota, and now Mrs. Pitts's cookies travel to picnics on the beach, the Apostle Islands, and waterfalls around Bayfield. They are sturdy cookies and hold up well on our adventures.

MAKES 36 COOKIES

1   cup butter, softened
2   cups sugar, plus more for rolling
2   eggs
1   teaspoon lemon extract
1   teaspoon orange extract
3   cups all-purpose flour
1   teaspoon cream of tartar
1   teaspoon baking soda
1   teaspoon kosher salt

Preheat oven to 350°F. In the bowl of a stand mixer fitted with the paddle attachment, cream butter and 2 cups sugar together on medium speed. Add eggs, one at a time, and then add lemon and orange extracts.

In a separate bowl, combine flour, cream of tartar, baking soda, and salt. Add dry ingredients to the butter mixture and mix until combined.

Place additional sugar on a plate and line a sheet tray with parchment. Roll the dough into quarter-sized balls, roll in sugar, place on sheet tray, and flatten with the palm of your hand. Bake until crispy, 10 to 12 minutes. Transfer cookies to a wire rack to cool.

Before the Ice

The waves broke and spread their waters swiftly over the shore. One
after another they massed themselves and fell; the spray tossed itself back with the energy
of their fall. The waves were steeped deep-blue save for a pattern of diamond-pointed light
on their backs which rippled as the backs of great horses ripple with muscles as they move.
The waves fell; withdrew and fell again, like the thud of a great beast stamping.

—Virgina Woolf, *The Waves*

AS WILL AND I PICKED OUR WAY ALONG SHORE in late November, the lake was restless—heaving itself on shore and instantly morphing into ice. The deafening roar of wind and water (literally—it was so windy I couldn't hear Will) was breathtaking and awe inspiring. Most days the lake is placid and its strength is cloaked under a liquid blue blanket, and while I know there's ferocity lurking under that cloak of civility, it's easy to forget that the lake is an elemental force to be reckoned with. Humility of spirit and communion with nature—two lessons learned on a blustery day in November.

The gulls were hovering overhead, diving and floating in the wind currents. Those white plastic boxes full of fish entrails, leftovers from cleaning the fish for market, were full of their version of an all-you-can-eat buffet—bits and parts of freshly caught fish.

We stayed out there, soaking wet and lightly frosted with ice, until streaks of yellow, orange, and pink lit up the sky. It was tough to leave—the light was extraordinary, the air was electrified, and the waves were relentless, but numb fingers won out and we hopped back in the car. The lake, in all its untamed power, is truly an inland sea. As I stood on the shore before we drove away, I understood my place in the "family of things" (as poet Mary Oliver would say), small but not insignificant. Each and every piece of the weave has its place, and mine is on the shores of Lake Superior.

Winter

SNOWSTORMS are one of my favorite things on this planet, and thankfully Bayfield delivers in spades. This is a good thing given that a large portion of our winter revolves around snow and its various uses: cross-country skiing, snowboarding, downhill skiing, and dog sledding . . . and as a picturesque backdrop for Vietnamese beef stew or gnocchi mac and cheese. Saunas are always better when it's cold, and the stars seem to burn brighter in the night sky when it's below zero outside. We start discussing the advent of the ice road between Bayfield and Madeline Island and look for the telltale line of Christmas trees that will mark the eventual route. Winter is our "down" season, when we have time for dinner parties, skijoring adventures, hikes to the ice caves, and catching up after a busy tourist season.

As Henry David Thoreau suggested we do, I've "resigned myself to the influence of the earth." Nature knows we need the quiet and rest of winter before the riotous bounty of summer begins again. I'm willing to follow the earth's lead and live in accordance with the ageless rhythms of such a wise spirit. Snowflakes, icicles, warm light from our porch casting shadows on the snow, long nights, saunas, the muffled quiet during a snowstorm, fires in the woodstove, the sound of ice on the lake, and the feeling of being tucked in for a "long winter's nap"—these are the reasons I appreciate the austere beauty of winter. After all, I know we'll be back at the beach soon enough (after we survive mud season).

Dougherty
Snow Day

WE WERE ALL LOOKING FORWARD to a snowy Sunday, but as the hours marched on toward Monday I started to lose hope. The weather people had been downgrading the storm all day, and by eight-thirty that night I had resigned myself to a measly dusting of snow (while my family in Minneapolis was literally rolling in it).

An hour later, we were celebrating. Jack came downstairs with the most marvelous news—a new winter storm warning had been issued and five to nine inches of snow was on the way. I love a snow day like George loves his Chuckit, and judging from Charlie's happy dance, he does as well. I couldn't wait to wake up on Monday morning to a world of white.

School was technically in session, but we live twelve miles away, the roads were bad, and it was still snowing when we woke up, so I decided a Dougherty Day was in order. (A Dougherty Day is an unplanned day off to lounge around the house and play hooky.) The previous week had been a blur—between ski team, volleyball, and rehearsals for our community theater's production of *A Christmas Carol*, we were running around constantly. This would be a much-needed break from the treadmill of commitments the kids have each week. We played with the dogs outside, went for a walk downtown, played cards, and then spent the afternoon in the kitchen baking cookies and assembling Christmas treats. It was a perfect snow day.

Snow Day Waffles

It was snowing, we were out of milk and bacon, the grocery store was closed, and the kids wanted waffles. This situation required some ingenuity in the baking department. After looking through a number of cookbooks, Meghan and I created these waffles based on what we had on hand. Now, if we could have created some bacon, it would have been an epic snow day breakfast!

MAKES ABOUT 8 BELGIAN-STYLE WAFFLES

2 cups flour
2 tablespoons brown sugar
2 tablespoons maple sugar
2 teaspoons baking powder
1 teaspoon baking soda
1 teaspoon kosher salt
2 eggs, lightly beaten
2 cups buttermilk
½ cup butter, melted and cooled
1 tablespoon vanilla

Combine flour, brown sugar, maple sugar, baking powder, baking soda, and salt in a large bowl and set aside. In another bowl, combine eggs, buttermilk, butter, and vanilla; pour over dry ingredients. Stir until just combined and pour into a hot waffle iron. Cook until golden brown and serve immediately.

Persimmon & Chestnut Bread

Quick breads are a quick way to make your kitchen smell like Martha Stewart is in the house! This one is particularly aromatic because of the combination of orange, nutmeg, and ginger in the batter. Fuyu persimmons are available from late fall through February; they look like orange tomatoes and are ready to eat when they are firm. As soon as I spy them at the grocery store, I know that the holidays can't be far behind.

3½ cups flour
2 cups sugar
2 teaspoons baking soda
1½ teaspoons salt
1 teaspoon freshly grated nutmeg
4 large eggs, lightly beaten
1 cup butter, melted and cooled
²⁄₃ cup spiced rum
½ cup orange juice
3 Fuyu persimmons, pureed
1 pear, pureed
1 tablespoon vanilla
1 cup dried cranberries
1 cup toasted and chopped chestnuts
¼ cup chopped crystallized ginger

Preheat oven to 350°F. Butter and flour 2 large or 7 small loaf pans. In a large mixing bowl, combine flour, sugar, baking soda, salt, and nutmeg. Add eggs, butter, rum, orange juice, persimmon puree, pear puree, and vanilla and mix thoroughly. Fold in the cranberries, chestnuts, and crystallized ginger. Divide batter among the pans and bake until a toothpick inserted in the middle of the loaf comes out clean, about an hour if using large loaf pans or 30 minutes if using small pans. This bread freezes beautifully; wrap it well and it'll keep in the freezer for up to 3 months.

Gingerbread Cookies

MAKES ABOUT 36 COOKIES

3½   cups all-purpose flour
3   teaspoons ground cinnamon
2½   teaspoons ground ginger
1½   teaspoons baking powder
¾   teaspoon ground allspice
¼   teaspoon ground cloves
¼   teaspoon kosher salt
1   cup plus 2 tablespoons butter
1   cup firmly packed dark brown sugar
½   cup sugar
1   large egg
1   tablespoon vanilla
¾   cup molasses

In a large bowl, combine flour, cinnamon, ginger, baking powder, allspice, cloves, and salt and set aside. In the bowl of a stand mixer, beat the butter and sugars together until the mixture appears light and fluffy. Add the egg and vanilla; mix to combine. Add the molasses and mix, scraping down the sides of the bowl if needed.

Add the dry ingredients to the bowl and combine thoroughly. Cover the bowl with plastic wrap and refrigerate until firm, at least 2 hours or up to 1 day ahead.

Preheat the oven to 350°F. Remove the dough and cut it in quarters. Place one quarter on a floured work surface and let sit for a few minutes to come to room temperature. Cover the remaining dough and place it back in the refrigerator.

Line a baking sheet with parchment paper. Roll out the dough to a ¼-inch thickness and use cookie cutters to cut out the cookies. Transfer to the prepared baking sheets. Bake until cookies begin to firm up and look crisp, 10 to 12 minutes. Remove from oven and let cool on the sheet 5 minutes, then transfer cookies to racks to cool completely.

Life at
Twenty Below

I wonder if the snow loves the trees and fields, that it kisses them so gently? And then it covers them up snug, you know, with a white quilt; and perhaps it says "Go to sleep, darlings, till the summer comes again.

—LEWIS CARROLL, *ALICE'S ADVENTURES IN WONDERLAND*
AND THROUGH THE LOOKING-GLASS

"ARCTIC VORTEX"—it's the catchphrase of the week. Evidently, there was a breach in the jet stream and some very cold Arctic air made a break for the Gulf of Mexico. On its way to the Gulf Coast, it spilled all sorts of snow and subzero temperatures across the country, and it was particularly generous with its frigid air deposit in northern Wisconsin. It was twenty below when I woke up, and it stayed well below zero all day. On a positive note, on days like this the dogs get right down to business when we go outside.

The kids didn't have school, and at about noon Will and I decided to leave Meghan and Charlie to their constant squabbling about the television and go on a photo safari around Bayfield. It was windy, cold, and snowy—perfect conditions for capturing photos about life when an Arctic vortex settles in for a visit.

Continued on next page

At one point Will looked at me and asked, "Why do our winter photo safaris always happen in life-threatening conditions?" I had a hard time answering because the wind was howling and pelting what little exposed skin I had with surprisingly sharp snowflakes. We hopped back into the car and considered taking the photos from inside—until we saw a turkey in an apple tree. There is nothing like a rare shot to get two cold photographers back outside.

When we got home, we hiked down to the stream that runs through our ravine. Running water was a welcome sight on such a frozen day. I stood and listened, filling my ears with the sounds of water moving underneath a blanket of snow. There is life and movement everywhere, from a turkey seeking shelter to a sailboat in its cradle "on the hard," outfitted with a wooden structure to withstand winter's cold and snow. It's all about adaptation, patience, and perseverance. Six months from now the summer solstice will be upon us, the trees will be cloaked in green, and the water will flow unimpeded by snow and ice. Sure, it's cold out, but life goes on, even at twenty below zero.

Gnocchi Mac & Cheese

Charlie and Meg built an elaborate snow fort (I guess it takes a snowstorm to get them to work together without fighting), Will and Sadie were the targets for their snowball assault, and George was leaping and bounding all over the place. When I got the call saying that school was canceled, my brain went immediately to "What's for dinner?" What's better on a snowy day than cheese and carbs? Save for a bottle of red wine, not much, in my opinion.

SERVES 8

 8 slices bacon, uncooked
 ¼ cup chopped yellow onion
 2 garlic cloves, minced
 3 pounds gnocchi (purchased or homemade)
 ¼ cup butter
 ¼ cup flour
 2 cups whole milk
 1 cup heavy cream
 2 teaspoons dry mustard (I use Colman's)
 1 teaspoon salt, plus more to taste
 1 teaspoon pepper
 ¾ cup shredded Havarti cheese
 ¾ cup shredded Swiss cheese
 ¾ cup shredded Fontina cheese
 1 egg, lightly beaten
 ½ cup chopped sun-dried tomatoes
 1 cup crumbled Ritz crackers

Preheat oven to 350°F and generously butter a 9x13-inch baking dish. Cook the bacon in a medium skillet until crisp, remove from pan, and set aside. In the same skillet, sauté the onions until golden brown, about 10 minutes. Add the garlic, cook until fragrant, and then remove the onions and garlic from the pan and set aside.

Cook the gnocchi according to package directions and then drain, reserving 1 cup of the cooking water. Rinse gnocchi with cold water and place in buttered dish.

Melt the butter in a medium saucepan and whisk in flour. Cook the flour/butter mixture until it thickens and starts to bubble, 2 to 3 minutes. Gradually add the milk, cream, mustard, 1 teaspoon salt, and pepper, whisking constantly, and cook until slightly thickened, about another 3 to 5 minutes. Gradually add all the cheeses and stir until melted and thoroughly combined.

Remove ¼ cup of the cheese sauce and slowly whisk it into the beaten egg. Pour the egg mixture back into the sauce. Add reserved bacon, onion/garlic mixture, and sun-dried tomatoes and stir to combine.

Pour the sauce over the gnocchi and stir to make sure the sauce is evenly distributed over the gnocchi (if the sauce is too thick, gradually add gnocchi cooking water until it loosens up). Sprinkle crumbled crackers over the top. Bake for about 30 minutes or until the cheese is golden and bubbly. Let it rest for about 10 minutes before serving.

Pork Vindaloo

The snow stopped falling in the night, and the temperatures had fallen into subzero territory. The kids had another snow day, and we slept late, stayed in our pajamas well into the morning, shoveled a path to the sauna, and kept the woodstove stoked. Winter arrived with a bang this year; we'd better buckle up and enjoy the ride (at least it's going to be a white Christmas).

Pork vindaloo's warm spices, tender meat, and tangy sauce are a panacea for subzero temperatures. Vindaloo is derived from a Portuguese dish called carne de vinha d'alhos, named for the three main ingredients, carne (pork), vinho (wine), and alhos (garlic). In the Western Indian state of Goa, which was under Portuguese rule for 450 years, the wine was replaced with vinegar and Indian spices were added. Traditional vindaloo recipes do not use tomatoes, but since I doubt I'll encounter a Goan anytime soon, I added them to the sauce. You can leave them out if you are going for a more traditional Goan vindaloo experience.

3 tablespoons red pepper flakes
2 teaspoons whole cumin seeds
2 teaspoons fenugreek seeds
1½ teaspoons cardamom seeds
1½ teaspoons whole brown mustard seeds
1 teaspoon black peppercorns
⅓ cup plus 2 tablespoons red wine vinegar, divided
1 cinnamon stick, broken into small pieces
2 teaspoons brown sugar
2 teaspoons kosher salt
1 cup coconut oil
2 medium yellow onions, sliced
6 tablespoons water, divided
  Whole head of garlic, peeled and separated
2-inch piece ginger, peeled and chopped
3 pounds pork, trimmed, cut into 1-inch cubes, and seasoned with salt and pepper
1 cup chicken broth
2 teaspoons turmeric
1 can (14.5 ounces) chopped tomatoes, undrained (I use Carmelina brand tomatoes)
1 small yellow onion, chopped
2-inch bundle of cilantro stems, tied with kitchen twine
¼ cup chopped cilantro
  Cooked basmati rice, for serving

Grind the red pepper flakes, cumin seeds, fenugreek seeds, cardamom seeds, mustard seeds, and peppercorns in a spice mill or using a mortar and pestle. Place the ground spices in a bowl. Add ⅓ cup of vinegar, cinnamon stick pieces, brown sugar, and salt. Set aside.

Heat the coconut oil in a large sauté pan over medium heat and add the sliced onions. Sauté the onions, stirring frequently, until they turn deep golden brown and crisp. Watch them carefully—you are going for crispy, not burned. Remove the onions with a slotted spoon and place them in a blender or food processor. Add 3 tablespoons of water and puree the onions. Add the onion puree to the spice mixture in the bowl.

In a blender or food processor, combine the garlic, ginger, and 3 tablespoons of water and blend until you have a smooth paste. Set aside.

In the skillet you used to cook the onions, cook the pork cubes, in small batches, until lightly browned on all sides. Place the cooked pork in a bowl and continue with the remaining pork cubes until all pork has been cooked. Set pork aside. Place the ginger/garlic mixture in the same pan and cook for a minute. Add chicken broth and turmeric and stir to combine.

In a slow cooker, combine the pork and any juices that accumulated in the bowl, tomatoes, chopped onion, cilantro stems, spice/onion mixture, and the ginger/garlic mixture. Cook on high for 4 to 5 hours. Just before serving, stir in remaining 2 tablespoons of red wine vinegar and cilantro. Serve over basmati rice.

Leg of Lamb with Cranberry and Quince Chutney

Quince: now that's a fruit you don't see much of in northern Wisconsin—unless you shop at the Chequamegon Food Co-op and you know the produce manager, who's willing to order them for you, by the case. So when a case of quince is sitting in your kitchen, it's time to get busy figuring out what to do with such a fancy fruit, and lamb is a good place to start. Pomegranate molasses, with its zippy tang, can also be hard to find in a little northern town, but it's worth seeking out next time you are near a Middle Eastern or Greek grocery store. I buy the Alwadi brand from Bill's Imports in Minneapolis, and a bottle lasts a long, long time. It's very concentrated, so a little goes a long way.

SERVES 8

1   5-pound boneless leg of lamb
    Kosher salt and freshly ground black
    pepper to taste
8   cloves garlic, peeled and halved crosswise
3   shallots, peeled and quartered crosswise
⅓   cup chopped rosemary, divided
¼   cup chopped fresh oregano, divided
6   small, firm, tart apples, divided (I use
    Granny Smith)
2   small sweet onions, quartered
1   medium bulb fennel, trimmed and cut
    into ¾-inch wedges
1   cup Cranberry and Quince Chutney
    (recipe follows), plus more for serving
1   cup apple cider
½   cup pomegranate molasses
    Zest and juice of 1 lemon

Preheat oven to 425°F. Tie lamb with kitchen twine in 1-inch intervals so it forms an even shape; season liberally with salt and pepper. Using a paring knife, pierce the meat in 8 places and stuff holes with the garlic, shallots, and half of the rosemary and oregano. Halve 2 apples crosswise, remove cores, and place apples, cut side down, in the bottom of a roasting pan. Add onion and fennel pieces and season with salt, pepper, and remaining rosemary and oregano. Place lamb on top of apples and vegetables.

Cut and core remaining apples and arrange cut side up around the lamb. Fill each apple with about 2 tablespoons Quince and Cranberry Chutney. Whisk together apple cider, pomegranate molasses, remaining chutney, and lemon zest and juice in a bowl; spread over the lamb and apples.

Place in oven and roast for 30 minutes. Reduce temperature to 325°F and continue to cook until an instant-read thermometer inserted into the thickest part of the lamb reads 130°F, about another 60 minutes for medium-rare. Remove lamb from the oven and let rest for 20 minutes. Remove twine and thinly slice lamb crosswise; transfer to a serving platter. Arrange apples, onion, and fennel alongside lamb. Serve with more Cranberry and Quince Chutney on the side.

Cranberry and Quince Chutney

Quince are in season from October through December. They are on the astringent side when raw but have a honey, floral quality when they are cooked and pair nicely with game and lamb. If you find yourself quince-less and don't want to hunt them down, you can substitute a tart apple.

MAKES ABOUT 4 PINTS

- 4 cups dark brown sugar
- 3 cups water
- 1½ pounds fresh or frozen cranberries
- 1½ pounds quince, peeled, cored, and diced into ½-inch pieces
- 3-inch piece of fresh ginger, peeled and grated
- ¼ cup chopped crystallized ginger
- ¼ teaspoon whole cloves
- Zest and juice of 1 lemon
- Zest and juice of 1 orange

In a large pot over medium-high heat, dissolve the sugar in the water. Add cranberries, chopped quince, grated ginger, crystallized ginger, cloves, lemon zest and juice, and orange zest and juice. Bring the mixture to a boil, then reduce heat to a simmer and cook until the quince is soft, the cranberries have popped, and the mixture has thickened slightly, about 45 minutes.

While the chutney is cooking, prepare the jars and lids for canning. Place 4 pint jars on rack in a large pot, add enough water to cover the jars, and bring to boil over high heat. Boil for 10 minutes, then turn off heat and allow jars to rest in the hot water. Meanwhile, put bands and lids in small saucepan and cover with water. Heat over medium heat until the water is simmering, then remove pan from heat and allow bands and lids to rest in hot water until ready to use.

Ladle hot chutney into hot sterilized jars, leaving ¼-inch headspace. Wipe rims of jars, cover with lids, and screw on bands until just barely tight. Place jars on rack in pot and cover completely with water. Cover pot and bring to a boil over high heat. Boil for 10 minutes. Turn off heat, uncover pot, and allow jars to rest in water for five minutes. Remove jars from pot and allow them to rest undisturbed on countertop for six hours or overnight.

Note: Home canning carries food safety risks. For complete canning instructions, consult the University of Wisconsin Extension's many publications on home canning and preserving (http://fyi.uwex.edu/safepreserving) or the National Center for Home Food Preservation's resources (http://nchfp.uga.edu).

Brie en Croute with Curried Nuts

My friend Ellen asked if I would like go caroling in Bayfield on Sunday. I'm tone-deaf, but it's Christmas, so anything goes, right? A group of hardy souls walked around Bayfield, in a snowstorm, and serenaded our neighbors. After the singing adventure, another friend, Liz, rang my doorbell bearing a gift bag full of treats, one of which was Sassy Nanny Holiday Brie. The caroling was magical, and the brie was the icing on the bûche de Noël. Since I'm all about going over the top, I thought curried nuts, cranberry and quince preserves, and puff pastry would be a good way to honor a limited-edition Brie.

SERVES 8 TO 10

2 tablespoons butter
¼ cup roughly chopped roasted, unsalted cashews
¼ cup roughly chopped roasted, unsalted pecans
¼ cup raw sugar
3 tablespoons curry powder
2 tablespoons maple sugar
Flour for rolling out
1 sheet puff pastry (I use Pepperidge Farm)
1 wheel Brie, top removed (I use Sassy Nanny Holiday Brie)
¼ cup Cranberry and Quince Chutney (see page 143; you can substitute any good and tart fruit preserves)
¼ cup minced peppadew peppers

Generously butter a dinner plate and set aside. In a sauté pan over medium-high heat, combine cashews and pecans, sugar, curry powder, and maple sugar and heat, stirring constantly, until the sugar has melted and the nuts are evenly coated. Place the nuts on the buttered plate and allow to cool. Once they have cooled down, break into bite-sized pieces and set aside.

Preheat oven to 375°F and cover a sheet tray with parchment. Flour your work surface. Roll out the thawed puff pastry on floured surface until it's about a 12-inch square. Place the Brie in the center of the dough; top with chutney, peppadews, and nut mixture. Bring the four corners of the puff pastry together and twist to seal. Place on prepared sheet tray and bake until the puff pastry is flaky and golden, about 30 minutes. Serve immediately with crackers.

Catching
Sea Smoke

MY FIRST EXPERIENCE WITH SEA SMOKE came in a bottle of Pinot Noir from California. But the real deal over Lake Superior is far more impressive. Sea smoke (or arctic fog) results from very cold arctic air moving over warmer water. As I watched it roll in on a frigid afternoon, I found it amazing to think that Lake Superior was at least 35 to 45 degrees warmer than the air. It had been an unbelievably cold December, the nighttime temperatures had been below zero for days, but the lake hadn't cooled down enough to freeze yet. And sea smoke was the result of the last remnants of summer warmth in the waters of the lake meeting the icy cold air of winter.

We've been inhabitants of northern Wisconsin long enough now to laugh in the face of subzero temperatures, put on our layers, wool socks, and mukluks, and head out for a sea smoke photo safari. We started in Bayfield but decided we should be a little more adventurous and head up toward Cornucopia to check out the open lake.

Driving north was a good call. The lake was stunning. Cornucopia is a quaint fishing village about twenty miles from Bayfield on Siskiwit Bay, with a farmers' market in the summer; Ehler's, an old-fashioned general store; and the (now famous) sea caves in Mawikwe Bay. Since the bay is open to Lake Superior, the vastness of the lake was palpable; the wind-driven waves were racing across the bay and sea smoke was twisting offshore. Yet another gift from the lake: a glimpse at the alchemy of air and water, imagined as dancing arctic fog.

Bacon and Pancetta Jam

Bacon jam. I'd never heard of such a wondrous thing until I did an internet search for "pork in a slow cooker recipe." And I owe the revelation to Martha Stewart. You'd think a woman like me, with a deep love for both pork and condiments, would have already jumped on the smoky-bacon-jam wagon, but I was a babe in the bacon woods. Martha's recipe was a little austere for my taste, but after I added pancetta, cranberries, thyme, and maple sugar, it was ready to take a place of pride in the condiment section of my refrigerator.

MAKES ABOUT 3 CUPS

1	pound good-quality bacon (I use Sixth Street Market Delta Diner bacon)
1	pound pancetta (I get mine at Northern Waters Smokehaus)
2	cups chopped yellow onion
1	cup chopped shallots
1½	teaspoons kosher salt
1½	teaspoons black pepper
4	cloves garlic, minced
1	cup fresh cranberries
1	cup very strong brewed coffee (I use Big Water's Sea Smoke Blend)
¾	cup maple syrup (I use 219 Syrup)
¾	cup apple cider vinegar
½	cup maple sugar (you can substitute brown sugar)
1	tablespoon chopped fresh thyme

Chop the bacon and pancetta into ½-inch pieces and sauté in a Dutch oven over medium heat until it's crispy and browned. Drain on paper towels and set aside. Remove all but 3 tablespoons of the drippings and return the pan to medium heat. Add the onions, shallots, salt, and pepper and sauté until softened, about 10 minutes. Add garlic and sauté until fragrant, about 1 minute.

Combine the pancetta/bacon mixture with all the remaining ingredients in the Dutch oven, lower the heat, and simmer for 45 minutes. Remove from heat, let cool for 10 minutes, and pulse in a food processor until it's a spreadable consistency. The bacon jam will keep for up to 3 weeks in the refrigerator in a covered container.

Moroccan Cheese Ball

Everyone needs a cheese ball in their repertoire; they are easy to put together and are a consistent crowd-pleaser (plus you can put the leftovers in an omelette the morning after the party). My experience with cheese balls was extensive but not terribly varied, primarily of the cheddar cheese/cream cheese/onion/chopped almonds variety. While those stalwart cheese balls have their place in the world, I like something with a little more pizzazz. Morocco seemed like a good place to find my snazzy cheese ball: warm, smoky spices; preserved lemons; and pistachios. Cheese ball perfection.

MAKES 1 CHEESE BALL

1   package (8 ounces) cream cheese, softened
1   package (8 ounces) goat cheese, softened
½   cup freshly shredded Parmesan cheese
1   tablespoon minced preserved lemon
    (see recipe on page 35)
½   cup chopped fresh cilantro
¼   cup minced dried apricots
1   teaspoon cumin
½   teaspoon cinnamon
¼   teaspoon cardamom
1   garlic clove, minced
1   teaspoon kosher salt
½   teaspoon cracked black pepper
½   cup coarsely ground pistachios
    Crackers or baguette, for serving

In the bowl of a stand mixer, beat together cream cheese, goat cheese, Parmesan cheese, and preserved lemon. Fold in the cilantro, apricots, spices, garlic, salt, and pepper and combine thoroughly.

Transfer cheese mixture to a piece of plastic wrap and shape into a ball. Cover with pistachios, pressing to adhere. Wrap ball in the plastic wrap and refrigerate for at least 2 hours or up to 24 hours. Serve with crackers or thinly sliced baguettes.

Poblano and Tomatillo Pork with Cheddar Grits

I remember when the kids were little, the period from 5 to 7 P.M. was nightmarish, with crabby kids rioting while I was trying to prepare dinner. Fast-forward twelve years, and 5 to 7 is still the witching hour. No crabby kids, just various drop-off/pickup assignments for four kids in three different sports. Dinner needs to be quick and ready when they get home or they may revert to their younger, riotous selves. Both the pork and grits need a little help at the start, but this is mostly hands-off for a majority of the cooking time—helpful when there are permission slips to sign and homework to review!

SERVES 8 TO 10

FOR THE PORK BRAISE

- 3 tablespoons olive or canola oil, divided
- 1 4- to 5-pound Boston butt pork shoulder, seasoned with salt and pepper
- 3 medium onions, chopped
- 4 garlic cloves, minced
- 6 poblanos, chopped, with seeds
- 2 pounds fresh tomatillos or two cans (11 ounces each) tomatillos
- 3 tablespoons cumin
- 1½ tablespoons Tajin Clásico seasoning
- 2 tablespoons chipotle powder
- 2 tablespoons ancho chile powder
- ½ teaspoon salt
- ¾ cup chopped fresh cilantro

FOR THE CHEDDAR GRITS

- 2 tablespoons butter
- ½ onion, chopped
- 2¾ cups water
- 2 cups whole milk
- 1¼ cup uncooked grits (I use Quaker Quick Grits)
- 1½ cups shredded sharp white cheddar
  Salt and pepper to taste

Heat 1 tablespoon of oil in a large Dutch oven over medium-high heat. Add pork shoulder and brown on all sides. Place meat in slow cooker. Add remaining 2 tablespoons oil to pan, add onions, garlic, and poblanos, and sauté until soft and onions are golden, 7 to 10 minutes. Add tomatillos, cumin, Tajin, chipotle powder, ancho powder, and salt and sauté for another 2 to 3 minutes. Use an immersion blender to puree the tomatillo mixture in the pan until smooth; alternatively, very carefully transfer the tomatillo mixture to a blender or food processor and puree until smooth. Pour pureed mixture over the pork in the slow cooker and cook on high for 6 hours.

To prepare the grits, heat butter over medium heat in a large saucepan; add the onions and sauté until softened and golden. Add water and milk and bring to a boil. Reduce heat to medium-low and slowly add the grits, stirring to combine. Cover and cook until thickened, 12 to 14 minutes. Add the shredded cheese and continue cooking until the cheese is melted, another 2 to 3 minutes. Taste and add salt and pepper if needed.

Just before serving, shred the pork and stir in the cilantro. Serve over hot cheddar grits.

Bacon, Onion, and Blue Cheese Yorkshire Pudding

Popovers are a Sunday morning favorite at our place, and one wintery morning I wondered what would happen if I made one big popover with smoky, peppery bacon, onions, and blue cheese. Kind of a riff on Yorkshire pudding, with bacon drippings in place of the beef drippings. It turns out that Sunday morning musings about bacon, blue cheese, and popover batter lead to a crispy, custardy, bacon-y pan of goodness.

SERVES 8

8	ounces peppered bacon
4	tablespoons butter
2	sweet onions, thinly sliced
1	teaspoon salt
4	eggs, beaten
2	cups flour
1½	cups whole milk
2	teaspoons dry mustard (I use Colman's)
1	tablespoon fresh thyme
4	ounces blue cheese, crumbled

Chop the bacon into 1-inch pieces and cook over medium heat until crisp, about 10 minutes. Remove the bacon from the pan and set aside. Pour the bacon grease into a 9x11-inch baking dish and set aside. Return the pan to medium heat and add the butter, onions, and salt. Cover the pan for 5 minutes to sweat the onions and then raise the heat to medium-high, uncover, and cook until lightly caramelized, another 5 to 7 minutes. Remove from heat and set aside.

Heat oven to 400°F. Whisk the eggs, flour, milk, mustard, and thyme in a bowl until thoroughly combined. Let the batter rest for 30 minutes at room temperature (this is important because it allows the gluten to relax, lets air bubbles escape, and allows the flour to absorb the liquid). After the batter has rested, place the baking dish (with the bacon grease) into the oven and heat for 10 minutes. Remove from oven and pour in the batter. Add onions, blue cheese, and bacon. Place in oven and bake until puffed and golden brown, about 30 minutes. Serve immediately.

Chicken Liver Pâté with Pancetta, Quince, and Calvados

I have a distinct memory of being a six-year-old at the dinner table with a plate full of liverwurst in front of me. I wasn't a fan of liverwurst then, and if memory serves me correctly, I didn't touch it. Fast-forward thirty-six years, and liverwurst has been reimagined as pâté; not only do I eat it with verve, I make it on a regular basis. I have to admit, my pâté bears very little resemblance to the Oscar Mayer liverwurst of my youth—it's not wrapped in yellow plastic, pancetta from Northern Waters Smokehaus plays a strong supporting role, quince adds a hint of floral sweetness, and chestnuts give it a satisfying crunch.

MAKES ABOUT 8 RAMEKINS OR 4 CUPS

3   containers (15 ounces each) fresh, all-natural chicken livers
¾   cup coarsely chopped chestnuts or hazelnuts
6   tablespoons olive oil
    Kosher salt
1   pound pancetta, cut into ¼-inch dice
3   shallots, minced
2   garlic cloves, minced
1   quince, peeled and cut into ¼-inch dice
1   teaspoon finely chopped rosemary
1   teaspoon finely chopped fresh thyme
1   cup Calvados
2   sticks butter, at room temperature
    Freshly ground black pepper
    Crackers or baguette for serving

Rinse the livers and trim off the tough tissue that connects the lobes; pat dry and set aside. In a sauté pan over medium-high heat, heat the nuts until they are fragrant and start to turn golden brown. Set aside.

In the same sauté pan you used for the nuts, heat the olive oil over medium-high heat and add the chicken livers, seasoning with a small amount of salt. Cook the livers, turning once or twice, to medium rare,

lightly browning on both sides, about 4 minutes. Set the livers aside and add the pancetta, shallots, garlic, quince, rosemary, and thyme to the pan. Gently sauté over medium heat until the pancetta is slightly colored and the shallots and quince are softened. Add the Calvados and deglaze the pan, scraping with a wooden spoon and cooking until the Calvados is reduced to about ⅓ cup. Set aside to cool slightly.

In a food processor, combine the cooled livers, pancetta mixture, and butter; process until well blended. Season with salt and pepper to taste. Line small bowls or ramekins with plastic wrap, equally divide the nuts among the bowls, and then add the pâté, lightly covering it with the plastic wrap. Refrigerate until set, about 6 hours. Grind additional pepper over the top before serving with crackers or slices of baguette. The pâté keeps for a week in the refrigerator and up to 3 months (well wrapped) in the freezer.

The Last
Ferry Ride

MY iPHONE BUZZED AND I READ THE ALERT from the Madeline Island Ferry Line: "Freeze up Update: Weather and ice conditions permitting, we hope to keep ferry service available through Tuesday January 6th. However, the winter storm moving in could cause cancellation of trips. We are expecting to have a reduced ferry schedule or windsled by Wednesday, January 7th. Get your supplies to the island and your vehicle to the mainland ASAP. We will update this message after 1 pm on Tuesday." January in Bayfield is quiet; the holidays are over, and winter, with its early evenings and snowstorms, settles in for an extended stay. The last ferry of the season is big news. The islanders need to tend to the logistics of life after the ferry stops running and before the ice road is safe enough for travel, and the mainlanders begin their speculation about the advent of the ice road.

I asked Ted if he wanted to catch the last ferry of the season and have lunch at the Beach Club on a subzero January afternoon. He was ready for the icy adventure, so we suited up and headed down to the ferry landing to catch the last ride of the season. I've ridden the ferry more times than I can count, but this ride was different: it was a sea of ice between Bayfield and Madeline, and I had to wonder how on earth we were going to get to the island.

The ride over was loud; the deep resonant thrum of the ferry motors and the steady drumbeat of ice and metal created a mind-numbing soundtrack. The ice chunks were six to eight inches thick and would bounce off the steel hull of the ferry and bob in the last sliver of liquid water we'd see until the end of March. The lake was freezing up fast, and the ice sheet was unbroken in every direction, except for the watery lane created by the ferry. In a couple of weeks, the ice road would be safe for vehicles and cars would be traveling where we were floating. And a few months after that, we'd be back to summer, with its blue water, sailboats, and ferry rides . . . a continuum of travel driven by Lake Superior and the many forms it takes as it moves through the seasons.

Asiago and Pear Ravioli

What do I do when it's below zero for days on end and snows, and snows, and snows? I begin a regimen of carbo-loading and go on a pasta bender. Ravioli freeze beautifully if you place them in a single layer on a sheet tray; once they're frozen, layer them with parchment paper inside a freezer bag. Having a batch of these stockpiled comes in handy when I have a hankering for pasta but have been outside skiing, hiking, skijoring, or simply freezing my face off because it won't stop snowing.

SERVES 4 TO 6

FOR THE PASTA DOUGH

- 3 cups Caputo "00" flour (you can substitute all-purpose flour), plus more for rolling out
- 4 eggs
- 1 teaspoon olive oil
- ½ teaspoon kosher salt
- 3–5 tablespoons water, divided

FOR THE FILLING

- 1 pound freshly shredded Asiago cheese
- 8 ounces mascarpone, at room temperature
- 3 pears, peeled, cored, and coarsely chopped
- 1 tablespoon minced shallot
- ½ teaspoon chopped fresh thyme
- ½ teaspoon kosher salt
- ¼ teaspoon black pepper

FOR THE CREAM SAUCE

- 1½ cups heavy cream
- 4 tablespoons butter
- 1 garlic clove
- ½ teaspoon salt, plus more to taste
- ¼ teaspoon coarsely ground black pepper, plus more to taste
  Pinch of red pepper flakes
- ½ cup freshly grated Parmesan cheese

In the bowl of a stand mixer, combine flour, eggs, oil, and salt. Turn the mixer on low and add 3 tablespoons of water. Add more water, 1 tablespoon at a time, until the mixture comes together and forms a ball. Knead the dough on a lightly floured board to make sure it is well mixed. Cover and set aside to rest for 30 minutes.

Combine all the filling ingredients in a bowl, mix to thoroughly combine, and refrigerate until you are ready to use.

Generously flour your work area. Cut the dough into 6 pieces and cover with a towel (don't cover the pasta with kitchen towels if you use a scented fabric softener because the pasta will pick up the scent—use parchment instead). With your hands, flatten and shape one piece of dough into a ½-inch-thick rectangle. Dust it lightly with flour and pass it through the widest setting on the pasta machine. If the dough comes out oddly shaped, reform into a rectangle. Fold it in thirds, like a letter, and if necessary flatten to ½ inch thick. Pass it through the widest setting again with the "seam" of the letter perpendicular to the rollers. Repeat this folding and rolling step three or four times, dusting the dough with flour if it becomes sticky.

Without folding the dough, pass it through the next narrowest setting on the pasta machine. Keep reducing the space between the rollers after each pass, lightly dusting the pasta with flour on both sides each time (I stop at setting number 6 on the KitchenAid pasta roller).

Dust a sheet tray with flour and set aside. Have a cup of water and a pastry brush nearby when you are ready to form the ravioli. Dust the work area and sheet of dough with flour. Lay out the long sheet of pasta and brush the top surface with the water. Drop tablespoon-sized scoops of the pear filling on the top half of the pasta sheet, about 2 inches apart. Brush the area between each mound of filling with water. Fold the other half of the dough over the filling like a blanket. Using your fingers, gently press out air pockets around each mound of filling. Use a sharp knife or a ravioli stamp to cut each pillow into individual ravioli and crimp the 3 edges with a fork to make a tight seal (if using a knife). Place the ravioli on a floured sheet tray and set aside to dry slightly while you assemble the remaining ravioli.

To make the cream sauce, combine cream, butter, garlic, 1/2 teaspoon salt, 1/4 teaspoon pepper, and red pepper flakes in a medium saucepan and cook over medium-low heat until slightly thickened, about 20 minutes. Add Parmesan and continue to cook until the cheese has melted. Taste and season with salt and pepper as needed.

Cook the ravioli in plenty of boiling salted water for 5 to 7 minutes (depending on how big they are). They'll float to the top when ready. Carefully lift the ravioli from water with a large strainer or slotted spoon. Serve immediately with cream sauce.

Al Capone's Roast

Food inspiration can strike at any time. For the annual Writers Read event at Northland College in Ashland, I made lunch on a January Saturday for all the regional writers who had bravely taken the stage and shared their stories about traveling and coming home. I sat down next to Rene, one of the writers, as lunch was winding down, and our conversation turned to food. We talked about Mount Royal (my favorite grocery store), Northern Waters Smokehaus (home of the best pancetta), and a sushi restaurant in a gas station in Duluth. Then Rene mentioned a Duluth meat market, Old World Meats, which makes a roast called Al Capone. A piece of stuffed beef named after a Mafia kingpin? That's a dinner idea for a snowy night that I can get behind.

SERVES 6

1	pound ground Italian sausage
4	tablespoons butter, divided
1	package (8 ounces) mushrooms, sliced
1	3- to 4-pound flank steak
8–10	oil-packed sun-dried tomatoes, chopped
6–8	pepperoncini, chopped (remove the seeds if you don't like it spicy)
½	cup pitted and chopped good-quality olives (use a mix; I like kalamatas, amfissa, and green olives)
12–14	basil leaves
2	garlic cloves, sliced
½	package (8 ounces) fresh mozzarella, sliced
½	cup shredded Romano cheese
	Tuscan Herb and Garlic Salt (see recipe on page 70)
	Freshly ground black pepper

Preheat oven to 375°F. In a sauté pan over medium-high heat, cook the Italian sausage until lightly browned and thoroughly cooked; set aside. In another sauté pan, melt 2 tablespoons of the butter and sauté the mushrooms until softened and browned, about 7 minutes. Set aside.

Place the steak on a cutting board and arrange it so the long edge runs perpendicular to you. Using a sharp knife and slicing parallel to your cutting board, butterfly the steak in half lengthwise. Make sure not to cut all the way through. (Leave a ½- to ¼-inch portion along the edge.) Fold open the meat like you would a book and flatten to form a rectangle. Using a meat mallet or rolling pin, pound the steak to a ¼-inch thickness

In a medium bowl, combine sun-dried tomatoes, pepperoncini, and olives. Place the flank steak on a flat surface with the grain running north and south (this will make it easier to slice after it's cooked). Layer with the ingredients as follows: Italian sausage, tomato/olive mixture, mushrooms, basil, garlic slices, mozzarella cheese, Romano cheese.

Roll up the flank steak as tightly as you can (don't worry if some of the filling comes out of the sides) and tie the roast tightly and securely with cotton twine. Liberally season the roast with herb salt and pepper. In a large cast-iron pan, melt remaining 2 tablespoons of butter and sear the roast, over medium-high heat, on all sides. Place the cast-iron pan in the oven and roast until the internal temperature reaches 160°F, about 1 hour.

Remove from the oven, cover, and let rest for 15 minutes. Slice and serve immediately.

Ice Caves Magic

Always in the big woods when you leave familiar ground and step off alone into a new place there will be, along with the feelings of curiosity and excitement, a little nagging of dread. It is the ancient fear of the unknown, and it is your first bond with the wilderness you are going into. What you are doing is exploring. You are undertaking the first experience, not of the place, but of yourself in that place. It is an experience of essential loneliness, for nobody can discover the world for anyone else. It is only after we have discovered it for ourselves that it becomes a common ground and a common bond, and we cease to be alone.

—WENDELL BERRY, *THE UNFORESEEN WILDERNESS*

JACK WAS LEAVING SOON, heading back to Madison for the second half of his freshman year. I wanted to do something epic: a collection of experiences he could take to Madison, package away in his dorm room, and pull out when he needed to remember why Lake Superior will always be home. A morning walk to the ice caves in a foot of fresh powder sounded pretty epic. We hopped in the car and drove about ten miles north of Bayfield, toward Cornucopia, for a hike along the frozen and cave-riddled shore.

While I'd been out to the ice caves twice in the past (in the company of approximately a hundred other travelers), this was the first time we traveled the mile or so alone. On the walk I felt a mixture of apprehension (how do I know if the ice is thick enough?), reverence (the snow, wind, and ice enveloped my eyes and ears), and excitement (Ted, Jack, and I were alone, walking across a frozen lake toward one of the wonders of this world).

There was a single track along the shore and out across the lake. It was quiet enough to hear the ice creak and pop with unseen swells from the lake, and it was solitary enough to feel the ancient energy radiating from the rocks that ringed the shore. Words can't begin to describe how it felt to witness the wild and ephemeral beauty of ice and sandstone. It was a work of art, created by wind and water—magical in its perfection.

Sharing the experience of sacred wisdom, imagined in ice and stone, with Jack and Ted was more than I hoped for when we set out. I know Jack carries that wisdom in his spirit, and a morning spent deepening his connection to this mystical place would serve him well as he moves into the world.

The last cave reminded me of a cathedral. The sandstone cliffs soared straight up, and the path through the crevasse led me about 150 feet back to the sound of running water. As I stopped and listened to the water deep in the belly of a sandstone cliff, I said a fervent prayer of gratitude. Grateful for a spirit that recognizes the divine in the sound of running water, for the unending blessings I've received over the course of my life, for the wisdom of wild places, for our children with their open hearts and a sense of wonder, for a partner who is my "ever-fixed mark," and for sandstone canvases painted with ice on the shores of my favorite lake.

Texas Red, or Seriously Good Chili

Chili is a reliable dinner option when we've been up at the "hill"—which is what we call Mount Ashwabay, our local ski area. From the day it opens sometime in December until the day it closes up shop in late March, you are guaranteed to find at least one Dougherty out there with skis or a snowboard strapped to their feet. Given the short days of winter, dinnertime comes quick, and having a pot of chili simmering in the oven while I'm cross-country skiing takes the pressure off.

SERVES 12 TO 14

12 dried japones chiles
8 dried guajillos chiles
6 dried New Mexico chiles
5 dried ancho chiles
8 pounds of beef chuck, cut in 1- to 2-inch cubes
  Salt and black pepper
6 tablespoons butter, divided, plus more if needed for browning the beef
4 onions, chopped
2 cans (28 ounces each) crushed tomatoes
12 cloves garlic, chopped
4 tablespoons cumin

4 teaspoons coriander
1½ teaspoons cinnamon
1½ teaspoons cloves
3 poblano chile peppers, seeded and chopped
2 Anaheim chile peppers, seeded and chopped
2 bottles (12 ounces each) of bock beer, plus more if needed
2 cups dark-roast brewed coffee (I like Big Water Snowplow Winter Blend)
1 can (7 ounces) chipotles en adobo
2 cups beef broth, plus more if needed
2 tablespoons kosher salt
1 disc (about 1.5 ounces) Taza guajillo Mexican chocolate
  Cheddar cheese, sour cream, and chopped green onions for serving

Slice all the dried chiles in half and remove the seeds. Heat the chiles in a dry sauté pan on medium heat for a couple of minutes on each side. Turn off the heat, add enough water to the skillet to cover the chiles, and let them soak for 45 minutes to an hour.

Place the cubed beef in a large bowl and season all over with salt and pepper. In a large sauté pan, heat 4 tablespoons of butter over medium-high heat. Add seasoned beef cubes to the pan. Working in three or four batches, brown the beef on all sides, adding additional butter to the pan if the pan looks dry. Set browned beef aside. In the same pan, cook onions until softened and golden brown, 7 to

10 minutes. Add tomatoes, garlic, cumin, coriander, cinnamon, and cloves and cook for 5 minutes. Remove from the pan and set aside.

Heat the large sauté pan that you cooked the beef and onions in over medium heat. Add the remaining 2 tablespoons butter and chopped poblano and Anaheim peppers; sauté until the peppers are softened but not browned, about 10 minutes. Lower the heat to medium and add the onion/spice mixture, beer, and coffee to the pan, stir to combine, and simmer for 5 minutes.

In a large Dutch oven or stockpot, combine the beef and any accumulated juices and the pepper/onion/beer/coffee mixture, and place on the stove over medium heat.

Drain the dried chiles that were soaking in the water and place in a blender with chipotles in their sauce and beef broth. Process until smooth and then add to the Dutch oven. Add salt. When chili begins to boil, turn heat down to low and let simmer, covered, for 5 hours or so, stirring occasionally. If it starts to look too dry, add more beer or beef broth.

About an hour before you plan to serve the chili, finely grate the Mexican chocolate and add it to the chili. Thoroughly mix to combine, remove the cover, and continue to simmer. Serve chili with sour cream, cheddar cheese, and chopped green onion.

Vietnamese Beef Stew

Traditional beef stew is hard to beat—it's hard to argue with hunks of meat basking in a red-wine-infused broth with carrots and potatoes, right? But if you're looking to shake things up a little, this beef stew inspired by pho is an excellent choice. And the cinnamon, ginger, and star anise flavors of the broth are perfectly suited to a cold and snowy evening.

SERVES 8

2 ounces dried shiitake mushrooms
1 cup boiling water
2 tablespoons butter, plus more if needed to brown the beef
2 pounds beef chuck, cut into 1-inch cubes and seasoned with salt and pepper
1 yellow onion, thinly sliced
1 jalapeño, roughly chopped with seeds
2 whole star anise
1 cinnamon stick
¼ cup brown sugar
¼ cup fish sauce
⅛ cup chili-garlic sauce
2 tablespoons oyster sauce
1 tablespoon rice vinegar
4 cups beef broth
3 garlic cloves, minced
⅛ cup minced fresh ginger
4 medium carrots, sliced into 1-inch rounds

Place shiitake in small bowl and add boiling water. Let stand until softened, at least 30 minutes, then drain mushrooms, reserving soaking liquid. Chop mushrooms and set aside.

Heat the butter in a large Dutch oven over medium-high heat. Brown beef cubes on all sides, working in batches and adding more butter to the pan if needed; set aside. Lower heat to medium, add onion, and sauté until softened and golden brown, about 10 minutes.

Add jalapeño, mushrooms, reserved mushroom liquid, star anise, and cinnamon stick to the pan, raise the heat to medium-high, and sauté until all the mushroom liquid has evaporated, about 5 minutes. Add brown sugar and cook, stirring often, until sugar is dissolved, about 2 minutes. Add the fish sauce, chili-garlic sauce, oyster sauce, and rice vinegar and cook, stirring and scraping the bottom of the pan, for about a minute. Add beef broth, reserved beef, garlic, and ginger and simmer, covered, over medium-low heat until beef is tender, about an hour. Add carrots and continue to simmer, uncovered, for an additional 20 minutes.

Ulf's
Curry Party

IF YOU HAD TOLD ME that there is a Norwegian soil scientist in northern Wisconsin who makes his own curry powder, I never would have believed you. However, over the past fifteen years, I've learned that anything is possible on the Bayfield peninsula and it's best to keep my mind open to all possibilities. Before moving here, I bought my curry powder in a jar at the grocery store, and while it always tasted a little flat compared to the curries we ate at our favorite Indian restaurant, I'd never considered making my own. So for years I settled for ordinary curry powder.

Like most things in Bayfield, my curry awakening started with an offhand remark. We were at a friend's for dinner, and I saw a quart-sized mason jar on her counter with "Ulf's Curry" scribbled on the lid. Being naturally nosy and kind of snarky, I asked what kind of Swede makes curry powder. Turns out in northern Wisconsin, not only do we have a curry-making Swede, but he throws an annual party in January (complete with a hot sauna) and everyone was invited.

My first curry party was a sensory smorgasbord: there were piles of deep golden turmeric, the earthy scent of cumin and cardamom filled the air, and I was in heaven. I sat at the table and peeled what felt like hundreds of cardamom pods and took it all in. I couldn't believe this was the community I was joining: a group of welcoming, interesting, curry-loving people on the shores of Lake Superior who loved curry enough to peel, grind, and chop their way through a cold January evening.

Ulf's recipe had evolved over about ten years, and by the time I arrived on the scene, the measuring and mixing had all the trappings of a precise operation, complete with a scale and measuring cups. The mixing was all theatrics, including music and cheering as the rivers of different spices joined to create the rich, golden color of the curry powder. A fine spiced mist hung in the air as the jars were filled. Over the years I've upped my allocation to 2 one-quart jars—there's nothing worse than running out of Ulf's curry in November with no hope of getting more until January.

When Jack came home from college one Thanksgiving break, I asked what he wanted for dinner, and he responded, "Ulf's curry." But we had a problem: my mason jar was empty. I called Ulf's partner, Pat, and asked her if she could scrounge up enough for a pot of chicken curry. And this is why I love living here: she said she was running low but would give me enough for a meal for my college freshman who had been eating cafeteria food for three months. I dropped off a bottle of Spanish wine in her kitchen and picked up my pint jar of Indian curry from the dining room table. Wine for curry—that's a bartering system I can believe in.

Curried Indian Meatballs

When Fred Faye, Bayfield farmer and Happy Hollow Creamery cheese maker, dropped off twenty pounds of ground lamb, I knew it was time to make a batch of Indian meatballs. There are a lot of opinions out there about the "perfect" meatball—on everything from the meat ratio to techniques for mixing and forming to whether to use ricotta or bread crumbs. I knew I wanted my meatballs to have enough substance to hold together when fried but also have a meltingly tender texture. I cobbled together a recipe and technique from the four hundred or so websites I visited. When the sauce came together with Ulf's curry powder and some red wine, I knew I had a winning dinner combination.

SERVES 10

FOR THE SAUCE

- 2 tablespoons vegetable oil
- 1 onion, minced
- 2 tablespoons chopped garlic
- 1 jalapeño, finely minced
- 2 bay leaves
- 3½ tablespoons curry powder
- 1 tablespoon dried oregano
  Salt and pepper, to taste
- 2 cans (28 ounces each) diced tomatoes, drained
- 1 can (15 ounces) tomato sauce
- 1 cup red wine
- 2 tablespoons tomato paste
- ½ cup roughly chopped cilantro
  Cooked basmati rice for serving

FOR THE MEATBALLS

- 1 pound ground beef
- 1 pound ground pork
- 1 pound ground lamb
- ¾ cup dried bread crumbs
- ¾ cup freshly grated Parmesan cheese
- ⅓ cup chopped fresh cilantro
- 6 tablespoons tamarind pulp
- 3 eggs, beaten
- 3 cloves garlic, finely minced
- 1-inch piece of fresh ginger, peeled and finely minced
- 3 tablespoons dried oregano
- 1 tablespoon fenugreek seeds
- 3 teaspoons kosher salt
- 1½ teaspoons red pepper flakes
- 2 tablespoons vegetable oil

To make the sauce, put 2 tablespoons vegetable oil in a Dutch oven and sauté the onion, garlic, and jalapeño until softened. Add the bay leaves, curry powder, oregano, and salt and pepper to taste and sauté for about 30 seconds. Add the drained tomatoes, tomato sauce, red wine, and tomato paste and simmer for 20 minutes. Keep sauce warm while you make the meatballs.

Combine the ground meats, bread crumbs, Parmesan, cilantro, tamarind pulp, eggs, garlic, ginger, oregano, fenugreek, salt, and red pepper flakes and mix with your hands until just combined—this will ensure you have a pillowy, tender texture. Form the mixture into 2-inch meatballs.

Heat 2 tablespoons oil in a large nonstick sauté pan over medium-high heat. Brown the meatballs on all sides and then reduce the heat to low and continue to cook until cooked through, about another 10 to 12 minutes. Add meatballs and ½ cup cilantro to the sauce and serve immediately with basmati rice.

Asian Meatballs with Ginger Soy Sauce

I've learned that there's a meatball for every kind of cuisine, and since I crave Thai and Asian flavors, this Asian meatball was a logical next step in my meatball journey. The brilliant thing about meatballs is their freezeability; I make a double or triple batch and freeze them for the nights when I don't feel like cooking but we want something hearty and delicious for dinner.

SERVES 4

FOR THE SAUCE

- 1 cup brown sugar
- 1 cup water
- ½ cup regular soy sauce
- ½ cup mushroom soy sauce (substitute regular soy sauce if you don't have mushroom soy)
- ½ cup hoisin
- ¼ cup rice vinegar
- ¼ cup sweetened black vinegar
- ¼ cup chili-garlic sauce
- ¼ cup oyster sauce
- ¼ cup peeled and chopped fresh ginger

FOR THE MEATBALLS

- ¾ cup dried bread crumbs
- ¼ cup whole milk
- ⅓ pound ground turkey
- ⅓ pound ground pork
- ⅓ pound ground chicken
- 4 green onions, thinly sliced
- 1 cup chopped fresh cilantro
- 1 egg, lightly beaten
- 2 tablespoons toasted sesame oil
- 2 tablespoons oyster sauce
- 2 tablespoons minced ginger
- 2 garlic cloves, minced
  Freshly ground black pepper
  Vegetable oil for frying
  Cooked white rice for serving

To make the sauce, combine brown sugar and water in a medium saucepan over medium-high heat and bring to a boil, stirring until the sugar dissolves completely. Reduce heat to medium-low and add both soy sauces, hoisin, rice vinegar, black vinegar, chili-garlic sauce, oyster sauce, and ginger. Simmer, stirring occasionally, until reduced by half, about 30 minutes. Keep sauce warm while you make the meatballs.

In a small bowl, combine bread crumbs and milk and stir to combine; let sit until the milk is absorbed, about 5 minutes. In a large bowl, mix turkey, pork, and chicken together until thoroughly combined. Add the milk-soaked bread crumbs, green onions, cilantro, egg, sesame oil, oyster sauce, ginger, garlic, and pepper to the meat mixture. Roll the mixture into 2-inch meatballs and set aside.

Put enough vegetable oil in a skillet to cover the bottom and heat over medium-high heat. Working in batches, brown meatballs until browned all over and cooked thoroughly, 8 to 10 minutes per batch. Serve immediately with white rice, spooning a little sauce over each meatball.

Italian Meatballs

My meatball adventure isn't over yet—there are still ham, Reuben, and Moroccan meatballs to discover—but my search for the perfect Italian meatball is over. During my research I read about using triple-ground meat to ensure a smooth meatball. For this recipe I ground the beef, pork, and lamb in my food processor and it worked like a charm, but you can also ask your butcher to triple grind the meat for you and save yourself a few dishes to wash.

One last tip before you start your own meatball journey: do not over-handle the meatball mix; gingerly form it into solid balls and then leave it alone. If you mold it, squeeze it, or smash it too much, the meatballs will be a much tougher consistency. The goal is a little pillowy-soft meatball, not a doorstop.

SERVES 10

- 2 pounds ground beef
- 1½ pounds ground pork
- ¾ pound ground lamb
- 2 cups dried bread crumbs
- 1 cup whole milk
- 3 eggs, lightly beaten
- 2½ cups whole-milk ricotta cheese, drained for 30 minutes in a cheesecloth-lined colander
- 1 cup freshly grated Parmesan cheese
- ¼ cup finely chopped fresh parsley
- 2 tablespoons kosher salt
- 1 tablespoon freshly ground pepper
- 1 tablespoon fennel seeds
- 1 tablespoon red pepper flakes
- ½ onion, minced
- 3 garlic cloves, minced
  Vegetable oil, for frying
  Marinara sauce and hot cooked spaghetti for serving

Combine beef, pork, and lamb in a bowl and mix well. Working in batches, grind the meat in a food processor until the texture looks smooth and you can't tell the difference between the meats, about 45 seconds. Place the ground meat back in the bowl and set aside.

In a small bowl, combine bread crumbs and milk; let sit until milk is absorbed, about 5 minutes. Add the milk-soaked bread crumbs, eggs, ricotta, Parmesan, parsley, salt, pepper, fennel seeds, red pepper flakes, onion, and garlic to the meat mixture. Roll the mixture into 2-inch meatballs and set aside.

Put enough vegetable oil in a skillet to cover the bottom and heat over medium-high heat. Working in batches, brown meatballs until browned all over and cooked thoroughly, 8 to 10 minutes per batch. Serve immediately with marinara and spaghetti.

Long Island
on Skis

EVERY FEBRUARY, THREE THOUSAND HARDY cross-country skiers head out over Chequamegon Bay toward Washburn for the Book Across the Bay race. Between the hundreds of candlelit ice luminaries and the concept of skiing over a frozen Lake Superior in the dark, my first Book Across the Bay was an evening I'll never forget. The next year we decided to book it LICC-style and headed out to Long Island for a winter version of Long Island Cocktail Club. Charly, the LICC czar, declared the ice safe and the island accessible, and we were badass enough to get ourselves, some tequila, hot dogs and brats, five kids, and two dogs over to Long Island for an afternoon adventure. It had been cold—I'm talking subzero temperatures—for many days in a row, and there was twenty inches of ice under our skis as we ventured across the frozen bay toward one of our favorite summer spots.

We skied nearly three miles to reach the island, but it was easy on the snow-covered ice. The wind picked up and a few snowflakes started to fall right before we got to camp, and I stopped and took it all in: darkening sky, shards of ice breaching the snow field, George and Zeus running up and down the trail, and a faint wisp of smoke from the camp Charly had already set up. It was mystifying to approach the point on skis instead of pulling up in our speedboat. The lake and the island seemed to be one, the usual beach-and-water boundary buried under a seamless white blanket.

The smoke from the chimney was a welcome sight, and Charlie and I were thinking about the Sixth Street Market brats I had packed for lunch. Skiing, even over flat surfaces, awakens a fierce hunger around lunchtime, and we quickened our pace as we got closer to camp. We were greeted by skis and snowmobiles on the snow-covered beach instead of the customary boats and paddleboards.

Near the end of our winter picnic, the snow began to fall in earnest, and we strapped on our skis and headed west, across the lake toward the Sioux Beach and home. Some of our crew had had the foresight to either a) not bring skis, thereby ensuring a ride to the beach, or b) be a child capable of a fair amount of complaining about having to ski back, thereby also ensuring a ride. Either way, Charly and crew went ahead of us, and as the sound of the engine died out, the muffled quiet of the falling snow filled my ears. It was a long but beautiful ski back to the beach—white in every direction and a frozen Lake Superior under my feet.

Blood Orange Marmalade

When I walk into the grocery store and spy a pile of blood oranges, I do a little happy dance. The season runs from December to March, and given my love of all things blood orange I wanted to find a way to preserve those midwinter gems. Marmalade is an easy way to save some midwinter sweetness.

I prefer the Moro variety, which are the most colorful of the blood oranges and have a stronger flavor than a normal orange, sweet with a hint of raspberry. Don't worry about the long soaking period; you won't lose any flavor, just the bitterness.

MAKES 4 HALF-PINT JARS

- 4 pounds blood oranges (about a dozen), peels left on
- 4 cups sugar
- 3 cups water, plus more to soak the oranges
- ¼ cup freshly squeezed lemon juice
- 1 tablespoon roughly chopped fresh thyme
- 1 cup bourbon

Using a fork or skewer, prick the oranges all over. Put the oranges in a large container, cover with water, and store in a cool place or the refrigerator. Change the water every day for 3 days. On the 4th day, remove oranges from the water, cut in half, and remove seeds. Thinly slice the oranges and chop them into small pieces.

Put the orange pieces, sugar, 3 cups water, lemon juice, and thyme in a heavy-bottomed pan and bring to a boil over high heat, then reduce heat. Cover and simmer for about 45 minutes. Add bourbon and continue to simmer, uncovered, for another 30 minutes.

While the marmalade is cooking, prepare the jars and lids for canning. Place 4 half-pint jars on rack in a large pot, add enough water to cover the jars, and bring to boil over high heat. Boil for 10 minutes, then turn off heat and allow jars to rest in the hot water. Meanwhile, put bands and lids in small saucepan and cover with water. Heat over medium heat until the water is simmering, then remove pan from heat and allow bands and lids to rest in hot water until ready to use.

Ladle hot marmalade into hot sterilized jars, leaving ¼-inch headspace. Wipe rims of jars, cover with lids, and screw on bands until just barely tight. Place jars on rack in pot and cover completely with water. Cover pot and bring to a boil over high heat. Boil for 10 minutes. Turn off heat, uncover pot, and allow jars to rest in water for five minutes. Remove jars from pot and allow them to rest undisturbed on countertop for 6 hours or overnight.

Note: Home canning carries food safety risks. For complete canning instructions, consult the University of Wisconsin Extension's many publications on home canning and preserving (http://fyi.uwex.edu/safepreserving) or the National Center for Home Food Preservation's resources (http://nchfp.uga.edu).

Olive Oil Thumbprint Cookies with Blood Orange Marmalade

These aren't your average vegan cookie. The combination of olive oil, thyme, and blood orange marmalade creates something seriously rich and savory. I like to add these to my cadre of Christmas cookies because they aren't terribly sweet, and they look festive with that garnet-colored marmalade nestled into each thumbprint.

MAKES ABOUT 4 DOZEN COOKIES

2½	cups flour
1¼	cups powdered sugar, divided
½	teaspoon baking soda
½	teaspoon salt
1	cup olive oil
4	teaspoons water, plus more as needed
4	teaspoons lemon juice
2	teaspoons lemon zest
2	teaspoons roughly chopped fresh thyme
¼	cup granulated sugar
1	cup Blood Orange Marmalade

Preheat the oven to 350°F and line a sheet tray with parchment. Combine flour, 1 cup of the powdered sugar, baking soda, and salt and set aside. In a separate bowl combine olive oil, water, lemon juice, lemon zest, and thyme and stir to combine thoroughly. Stir the liquid mixture into the dry ingredients just until well combined; if the mixture is dry, add a little more water.

Put the granulated sugar in a shallow bowl. Using about a tablespoon amount for each, roll dough into balls and then roll balls in sugar. Place the balls on sheet tray and flatten slightly with the bottom of a cup. Make an imprint in each one with your thumb and spoon in about 1 teaspoon marmalade. Bake until lightly browned, 10 to 12 minutes, and then let cool on a wire rack. Sprinkle with the remaining powdered sugar after they are completely cooled.

Sled Dogs
and Skijoring

LAST WEEK BROUGHT A SUNNY, warm-ish early March afternoon spent with some of my favorite people—and dogs—in the world.

It's hard to believe that I know enough sled dogs now to be able to declare one a favorite, but Vader is my guy. I met him eight years ago at Good Thyme, when Julie and Charly brought the dogs to the restaurant for a dog-sledding field trip for Meghan's class. I barely knew Julie then, let alone her pack of what seemed to me to be feral sled dogs, but as I watched them pull the kids around, I fell in love with their smiling faces. Vader, the blue-eyed devil, is a mixture of Robert De Niro and Hugh Grant, a goofy badass who wants to believe he's the emperor of the universe. Thank God for Pronce, his copilot; he's

all Sean Penn (in the *Fast Times at Ridgemont High* era) and is usually content with running next to a wanna-be emperor.

Since then I've also become a big fan of the Apostle Islands Sled Dog Race, an annual event in Bayfield that attracts thousands of spectators on the first weekend in February. Julie and Charly have been involved since the early days of this event, which is now in its twenty-second year and features two main races: a ten-dog, eighty-mile run, and a six-dog, sixty-mile run. There's also a forty-mile Sportsmen's Race, a Family Race, and a Youth Race (sixteen and under). After spending one cold and snowy Saturday at the chute where the mushers and pups take off, I was inspired to try a little dog-powered transportation.

As luck would have it, the next week Julie invited us out for a skijoring photo safari. Skijoring is like dog-sledding lite—there wasn't a sled or a team of howling pups raring to go, just one happy Siberian husky, a leash attached to my waist, and a pair of cross-country skis strapped to my feet. It's far less intense than managing a sled dog team but just as fun—the dog helps pull you along, but with only one pup, there's little chance for chaos. It was an afternoon for the record books and another reason I thank my lucky stars that I ended up in Bayfield with the greatest group of friends and dogs a girl could hope for.

Roasted Garlic Squash Soup with Apples and Boursin

A good old-fashioned snowstorm makes me happy, and a pot of soup on the stove during a snowstorm seals the deal as far as I'm concerned. Lucky for me, there's plenty of both snow and soup in Bayfield, land of the epic winter.

I always double my soup recipes so I have enough to freeze. If you're not a fan of frozen soup, just reduce all the ingredients here by half. (But you may want to rethink your position on frozen soup; you'll be glad to have it on hand when the next blizzard rolls in.)

SERVES 8, WITH PLENTY
LEFT OVER TO FREEZE

1	pound pancetta or bacon, chopped
½	cup butter
3½	cups chopped sweet onion
1	5- to 6-pound butternut squash, peeled, seeded and chopped into 2-inch pieces
3	medium apples, peeled and chopped
3	heads roasted garlic
2	tablespoons chopped fresh thyme
1	tablespoon minced fresh sage
3	tablespoons all-purpose flour
10	cups chicken broth
4	packages (5.2 ounces each) Boursin Garlic and Fine Herbs Gournay Cheese
4	teaspoons kosher salt
3	teaspoons coarse black pepper
1	tablespoon sriracha, plus more to taste

Place the pancetta in a large Dutch oven or stockpot and cook over medium heat until crispy and fully rendered. Remove the pancetta from the pan and set aside. Remove the fat from the pan and reserve. Add the butter to the pan and lower the heat to medium-low. Add the onion and cook until softened, 5 to 7 minutes. Add the butternut squash, apples, roasted garlic cloves, thyme, and sage, stir to combine, and cook for 15 minutes. Add the flour, stir to combine, and cook for 2 to 3 minutes. Add the chicken broth and bring to a boil. Turn down the heat to low, cover, and simmer until the squash is very soft, 20 to 30 minutes. Carefully puree, using a handheld immersion blender or a regular blender, until smooth.

Return the pureed soup to the pot and add the cooked pancetta, Boursin, salt, pepper, and sriracha, stir to thoroughly combine, and simmer for 10 minutes. Taste for seasoning and serve immediately.

Hot and Sour Soup with Fried Wonton Strips

SERVES 8

FOR THE FRIED WONTON STRIPS

½   of 18-ounce package egg roll wrappers

3   cups vegetable oil

FOR THE SOUP

2   tablespoons vegetable oil

8   ounces ground pork

6   green onions (white and green parts), chopped, plus more for garnish

4   garlic cloves, minced

3   tablespoons minced fresh ginger

6   cups chicken stock (preferably home-made or low sodium)

1   package (8 ounces) white button mushrooms, sliced

1   can (5 ounces) bamboo shoots, drained and rinsed

⅔   cup black vinegar, plus more if desired

5   tablespoons soy sauce, plus more if desired

2   tablespoons cooking sake

1½ tablespoons chili-garlic sauce, plus more if desired

1   tablespoon sesame oil

1   tablespoon sriracha

1   teaspoon light brown sugar

1   teaspoon black pepper

2   large eggs

1   cup chopped cilantro, for garnish

6   green onions, sliced, for garnish

To make the fried wonton strips, slice egg roll wrappers into ¾-inch-wide strips. Heat vegetable oil to an even simmer over medium-high heat. Add wrappers to the pan, being careful not to overcrowd them, and watch them carefully—they burn very

quickly. Remove wonton strips from oil when the strips are a golden brown and drain on paper towels. Set aside while preparing the soup.

In a large saucepan, heat oil over medium-high heat. Add pork, green onions, garlic, and ginger and cook, stirring and breaking the pork into smaller pieces, until the pork is cooked thoroughly, about 10 minutes. Add stock, mushrooms, bamboo shoots, vinegar, soy sauce, sake, chili-garlic sauce, sesame oil, sriracha, brown sugar, and pepper. Simmer for about 30 minutes and taste for seasonings. Add more chili-garlic if you want it hotter; add more vinegar if you want it more sour.

In a bowl, whisk the eggs and add them to the soup in a steady stream, stirring continuously. Serve immediately with fried wonton strips, cilantro, and green onions.

Vietnamese Pho Noodle Soup

Pho is a little word for a big flavor bomb of a soup filled with noodles, beef, dried spices, fresh herbs, and a healthy dose of hoisin and sriracha sauce. Ted, a self-professed pho aficionado, tells a tale of how he and his friend Rick traveled the length and breadth of the Twin Cities in search of the best bowl of pho they could get their hands on. I'm not sure what all the criteria (or their credentials) were, but I do know a restaurant with bullet holes in the wall was awarded extra points. So when I set out to make a batch, I knew I had an in-house expert to guide me to my own personal best bowl of pho.

The broth takes a little while to come together (don't skip the parboil for the bones; it makes for a much clearer broth), but after I micromanaged the broth and skimmed away most of the impurities (requiring about thirty minutes of standing at the stove and skimming), it was a breeze. Since I stock up at the Asian grocery store when I'm back in Minneapolis, I had a bag of fresh noodles in the refrigerator, but dried noodles will work just as well. After a couple of attempts at pho greatness, Ted said I nailed it.

SERVES 8, WITH PLENTY OF EXTRA TO FREEZE

FOR THE BROTH

- 2 large yellow onions, halved
- 6-inch piece of fresh ginger, halved lengthwise
- 1/4 cup vegetable oil
- 5–6 pounds grass-fed beef bones
- 3 pounds oxtails
- 6 quarts water
- 1 cinnamon stick
- 1 tablespoon coriander seeds
- 1 tablespoon fennel seeds
- 6 whole star anise
- 4 whole cloves
- 1 cardamom pod
- 1-inch chunk of yellow rock sugar (can substitute 10 ounces white sugar)
- 1/4 cup fish sauce
- 1 1/2 tablespoons kosher salt
  Beef broth, if needed

THE GOOD STUFF FOR THE BOWLS

- 1/2 pound flank steak
- 2 pounds rice noodles (I used fresh)
- 1/2 cup chopped fresh mint
- 1/2 cup chopped fresh cilantro
- 1/2 cup chopped fresh basil
- 1/2 cup thinly sliced green onions
- 2 limes, cut into wedges
- 2 or 3 chili peppers, sliced
- 2 cups bean sprouts
  Hoisin sauce (I like Lee Kum Kee)
  Sriracha hot sauce

Turn your broiler on high and move oven rack to the highest position. Place onions and ginger on baking sheet. Brush the cut sides with vegetable oil. Broil, turning occasionally, until charred on all surfaces, about 25 minutes total. Set aside.

While the ginger and onion are in the oven, fill a large pot (12-quart capacity works well) with cool water. Bring water to a boil and then add the bones and oxtails, keeping the heat on high. Boil vigorously for 10 minutes. Drain, rinse the bones, and rinse out the pot. Refill pot with bones and 6 quarts cool water. Bring to boil over high heat and lower to a simmer. Using a ladle or a fine mesh strainer, remove any scum that rises to the top. This is an important step—don't skip it!

Put the cinnamon stick, coriander, fennel, star anise, cloves, and cardamom pod in a fine-mesh bag and tie closed (I bought a reusable tea bag at the co-op). Add the bag of spices, charred ginger and onion, sugar, fish sauce, and salt to the broth and simmer, uncovered, for 4 to 5 hours. Strain broth through a fine-mesh sieve and then return the broth to the pot. Carefully skim fat off the surface of broth and discard.

Taste broth and adjust seasoning; add fish sauce, salt, and/or sugar if the broth tastes weak; add plain beef broth (homemade or canned) if it tastes too strong.

To prepare "The Good Stuff": Slice flank steak as thin as possible (try freezing for 15 minutes prior to slicing to make this easier). Follow the directions on your package of noodles—each brand is different. After the noodles are cooked, rinse thoroughly in cold water to keep them from sticking. Arrange steak and all other ingredients on a platter for the table. Your guests will "assemble" their own bowls.

When ready to serve, bring the broth back to a boil. Have guests fill their serving bowl with rice noodles and raw meat slices. Ladle boiling broth into each bowl; the hot broth will cook the raw beef slices. Guests can then add Good Stuff to their bowls. Serve immediately.

An Ice Road Ride

EVERY YEAR, ONCE THE BAY HAS FROZEN, a row of Christmas trees appears on the ice between Bayfield and Madeline Island marking the path of the eventual ice road. They're a sign that soon there will be a two-mile ice road connecting Madeline with the mainland. And in between the trees' appearance and the official decree that the road is closed a few months later, the ice road is a hot topic around town: usually either along the lines of a) "Is there going to be an ice road this year?" or b) "Is the ice road still open?" In between those conversational poles, cars travel back and forth and enjoy free and easy access to Madeline or the mainland.

I had ridden along many times on the ice road ride, but I had never piloted my own car across the frozen expanse of Lake Superior until one recent February. Since Ted had gone skiing with Jack and Charlie at Whitecap, it was up to me to get the car—with windows down and seatbelts off, in case we needed to make a quick escape—across the ice for a Sunday photo safari with Will and George. I called a friend to inquire about pointers for our voyage; she said to drive slow and stay between the orange cones (the road had cracked earlier in the week, and it had been rerouted prior to opening). I followed her directions to a T, and we made it across in one piece.

Midway through my inaugural voyage, we stopped to take photos of the ice beneath our feet (and tires). To my inexperienced eyes it looked thick enough, but when I heard the creaking that accompanies a passing car, I remembered that there was two hundred feet of water beneath me, and we quickly continued on our way.

When it was time to head back, my first thought was, "What time does the ferry leave?" But for once we could leave whenever we wanted—a pretty unusual feeling when you're on Madeline Island. We rolled down our windows, unbuckled our seatbelts, and pointed the car toward Bayfield and home.

Winter Salad with Apple Essence Dressing

My friend Ellen gave me a jar of apple essence (basically cider boiled down to molasses consistency), and I fell in love. It tastes like sweet/tart apple cider but in the form of a rich and deeply flavored syrup. I've used it in all sorts of ways, but my favorite so far is in the dressing for this winter salad—it has just enough of the sweetness and bite of apple cider to add complexity to my salad dressing.

Apple essence takes a couple of hours to prepare, so plan accordingly. It will keep for two to three months in the refrigerator; if you can it, it will keep indefinitely in your pantry. It will become your secret weapon in the kitchen, always on hand to make a kick-ass salad dressing. And who doesn't need that in their quiver?

SERVES 6

FOR THE APPLE ESSENCE

1   gallon fresh apple cider (from the refrigerated section; do not use shelf-stable apple cider)

FOR THE SALAD

6   carrots, peeled and sliced lengthwise into 4-inch pieces
2   tablespoons olive oil
1   tablespoon plus 1 teaspoon kosher salt, divided
2   teaspoons black pepper, divided
1   bag (9 ounces) fresh spinach
1   apple (Gala or Cortland), sliced
½   head red cabbage, thinly sliced
½   red onion, thinly sliced
½   cup crumbled Gorgonzola
1½ cups extra-virgin olive oil
¾   cup sherry vinegar (can substitute apple cider vinegar)
¼   cup apple essence
¼   cup maple syrup
2   garlic cloves, minced
2   tablespoons Dijon mustard

Pour a gallon of fresh apple cider in a heavy-bottomed stockpot or Dutch oven and heat to a boil over medium-high heat. Reduce heat to medium-low and simmer, uncovered, for 2 to 3 hours, stirring occasionally. The apple essence is ready when it has reduced to about 2 cups and coats the back of a spoon. Place in a clean container and store in the refrigerator.

Preheat oven to 400°F and line a sheet tray with parchment. Toss carrots with olive oil, 1 teaspoon salt, and ½ teaspoon pepper. Spread on sheet tray. Roast until browned and tender, about 40 minutes. Set aside.

Place the spinach, apple, cabbage, red onion, roasted carrots, and Gorgonzola in a salad bowl and toss to combine. In a medium bowl, combine olive oil, sherry vinegar, ¼ cup apple essence, maple syrup, garlic, Dijon, and remaining salt and pepper. Whisk vigorously to thoroughly combine and pour the dressing over the salad. Serve immediately.

Beefy Pies with Stilton and Stout

Ice caves, ice roads, cross-country skiing, and dogsledding: all happy by-products of our fantastically cold and snowy winters. With the right amount of layering and warm boots, winter has secured a place in my heart with its abbreviated daylight and crystal-clear, star-strewn night sky. While there's nothing like the lazy days of summer, the winter days are precious because the light is fleeting and night is so very long this time of year. Subzero temperatures and a five o'clock sunset always turn my mind to comfort food, and this crock of beef, cheese, and beer, covered with buttery puff pastry, is the perfect companion to February in Bayfield. I use individual oven-proof bowls/ramekins for this meal; the size of your container will determine how many beefy pot pies you'll end up with. This feeds a crowd, but you can divide the beef filling to suit your needs. The filling freezes nicely and can be stored away for future dinners on a cold night!

SERVES 10

1½ sticks butter, divided

4 pounds beef chuck roast, cut into 1-inch cubes and seasoned with salt and pepper

2½ large red onions, sliced

3 bottles (12 ounces each) stout beer

6 cloves garlic, finely chopped

¾ cup flour

6 cups beef stock, divided

4 teaspoons dry mustard (I use Colman's)

6 carrots, peeled and thickly sliced

6 stalks celery, thickly sliced

1 can (28 ounces) chopped tomatoes in puree

¼ cup chopped fresh rosemary

2 bay leaves

2 packages (8 ounces each) mushrooms, quartered

2 packages (17 ounces each) puff pastry (4 sheets; I use Pepperidge Farms)

1 package (16 ounces) frozen peas

1 pound Stilton cheese, crumbled

1 egg, lightly beaten

Heat 4 tablespoons butter in a large sauté pan. Working in batches, brown the beef on all sides. Transfer meat to a large Dutch oven.

Melt 4 tablespoons of butter in the sauté pan over medium heat, add onions, and sauté for 10 minutes.

Add beer and garlic, raise the heat to medium-high, and cook until nearly dry, about 20 minutes. After the beer has reduced, add flour to the onions and garlic and cook for 2 to 3 minutes. Slowly add 2 cups of beef stock and dry mustard and stir until thoroughly combined. Cook until slightly thickened, about 10 minutes. Add this mixture to the Dutch oven with the beef. Add carrots, celery, tomatoes, rosemary, bay leaves, and remaining 4 cups of stock to the Dutch oven and simmer for 2 hours.

While the stew is simmering, melt the remaining 4 tablespoons butter in a large sauté pan and sauté mushrooms over medium-high heat until softened and evenly browned, 5 to 7 minutes. Set aside.

Right before the stew has finished simmering, roll out the puff pastries into 12-inch squares and cut ten 6- to 8-inch circles (depending on how large your individual crocks are). Cover pastry and set aside. Add sautéed mushrooms, peas, and crumbled Stilton to the stew and stir to combine.

Preheat oven to 375°F. Divide the beef mixture among 10 individual crocks or pie tins. Place the puff pastry circles on the crocks and press the edges to seal. Cut slits into the pastry and brush with beaten egg. Bake until browned, about 45 minutes. Serve immediately.

Roasted Beef Marrow with Parsley and Caper Pesto

I ordered roasted veal marrow for the first time at Lake Avenue Café in Duluth. In the book *My Last Supper*, which asks famous chefs to describe their last meal, Anthony Bourdain answers, "Roast bone marrow with parsley and caper salad, with a few toasted slices of baguette and some good sea salt." If it was good enough for Bourdain's last meal, I thought it would be sublime for my Friday night dinner. I was tremendously glad I ordered it; the marrow tasted like beefy butter, and the tangy parsley and caper pesto was the perfect counterpoint to its rich and subtle sweetness.

As we were leaving the restaurant, I knew I wanted to try to make the dish at home, but I wasn't sure where to procure veal bones in Bayfield. I buy dog bones at the IGA, but I figured I would have a higher chance of getting Ted to slather his toasted baguette with marrow if it came in a different package than George's bones. I called Mount Royal, my favorite grocery store in Duluth, and sure enough, they had beef bones and were open until midnight. (This is when I knew I had some of the very best friends in the world, as they agreed to be dragged along on my marrow quest at 11 o'clock that same night.)

SERVES 6

- 8   3- or 4-inch-long pieces beef marrow bones
      Maldon sea salt and freshly ground black pepper
- 1   cup rough chopped fresh flat-leaf parsley
- 2   small shallots, chopped
- 2   garlic cloves
- 2   tablespoons extra-virgin olive oil
- 1½ tablespoons salted capers, rinsed
- 1   tablespoon fresh lemon juice
- ½   cup freshly grated Parmesan cheese for serving
- 8–10 slices baguette, brushed with olive oil and toasted, for serving

Preheat oven to 450°F. Place bones, wider cut side down, in a roasting pan. Season with salt and pepper. Roast bones until marrow is soft and begins to separate from the bone but before it begins to melt, 15 to 20 minutes depending on thickness of bones.

Meanwhile, place parsley, shallots, garlic, oil, capers, and lemon juice in a food processor or blender and process until smooth. Season pesto with salt and pepper.

Serve the bones, pesto, Parmesan cheese, and toasted baguette slices on a platter with salt and pepper on the side. Using a long, thin spoon, scoop marrow onto toast, top with pesto, and garnish with a pinch or two of salt and Parmesan. Serve immediately.

Apple Strudel Cheesecake

The birthday deal in the Dougherty house is simple: the birthday boy or girl gets to pick out the dinner, and the cake is served on the bright red "You Are Special Today" plate. That plate has seen a lot of cake: angel food with a simple icing, Black Forest with real maraschino cherries, Dairy Queen ice cream cake, and more bakery cakes with that super sweet frosting than I can count. But what comes flooding back every time I pull it out of the cupboard are the memories of my kid's faces behind the lit candles. Time picks up speed as our family grows up and traditions become more important—they offer a chance to bring the past forward and to create a foundation for the future.

SERVES 10

FOR THE CRUST

- ½ cup butter, melted, plus more for buttering pan
- 1 box (16 ounces) of gingersnaps, finely ground in a food processor

FOR THE TOPPING

- ⅓ cup light brown sugar
- ¼ cup flour
- 3 tablespoons butter, melted
- 1 teaspoon cinnamon
- ¼ teaspoon nutmeg
- ¼ teaspoon ground cloves
- ¼ teaspoon ground ginger
- ¼ teaspoon salt

FOR THE CHEESECAKE

- 3 packages (8 ounces each) cream cheese, softened
- 1 cup sugar
- 1 tablespoon vanilla
- 3 large eggs
- 3 or 4 tart apples, peeled and sliced
  Rum Caramel Sauce (see recipe on page 106)

Put oven rack in middle position and preheat oven to 350°F. Butter the bottom and side of a 9-inch springform pan.

Stir together cookie crumbs and ½ cup melted butter in a bowl. Reserve ¼ cup of the crumb mixture for sprinkling over cheesecake. Pat the remainder of crumb mixture into the bottom and up the sides of the prepared pan (about 1 inch thick). Put pan on a sheet tray and bake for 10 minutes. Set aside on a rack and allow to cool completely, about 25 minutes. Leave oven on at 350°F.

Combine topping ingredients in a medium bowl, mix to thoroughly combine, and set aside.

Beat cream cheese, sugar, and vanilla in a large bowl with an electric mixer at medium-high speed until fluffy, about 3 minutes. Add eggs one at a time, beating well after each addition. Pour into pan. Top with the apple slices in a spiral pattern. Sprinkle with topping. Bake until set, about 45 minutes. Chill for at least 2 hours before serving. Serve with caramel sauce.

Houghton Falls
Magic

IT WAS THE PERFECT DAY for a photo safari, but Will and I were fresh out of ideas. There was at least three feet of snow on the ground, and while I'm all for an adventure, slogging through thigh-deep snow sounded a little ambitious for me. But since all good things come to people who are indecisive, Julie suggested we check out Houghton Falls, where the river had backed up, frozen, and then made a break for the lake through a recently unfrozen railroad culvert. The result, she said, was huge sheets of ice hanging in the trees.

Will and I packed up George and Ted and headed out. We hiked back toward the lake and slid down into the ravine. There wasn't an ice sheet to be seen, though we saw lots of mossy harbingers of spring growing on the brownstone walls. I thought I must have misunderstood Julie because everything looked as it should: a snowy, ice-covered river winding through the brownstone, delicate and tenacious moss and spider webs, and the cedars, hemlocks, and birches overlooking the riverbed. And then I heard Ted say, "You've got to see this, it's unbelievable."

Huge ice sheets hung from the trees and littered the ravine floor. In the midst of the sheer massiveness of the chunks of ice, there were the most beautiful, delicate icicles coating the trees, the rocks, and the undersides of the ice sheets. We spent a few hours capturing the magic of water when it changes into ice.

Winter is tough in northern Wisconsin, but afternoons like that one more than make up for the mind- and body-numbing cold and snow. It was magical.

Epilogue

The world begins at a kitchen table. No matter what,
we must eat to live.

The gifts of earth are brought and prepared, set on the
table. So it has been since creation, and it will go on.

We chase chickens or dogs away from it. Babies teethe
at the corners. They scrape their knees under it.

It is here that children are given instructions on what
it means to be human. We make men at it,
we make women.

At this table we gossip, recall enemies and the ghosts
of lovers.

Our dreams drink coffee with us as they put their arms
around our children. They laugh with us at our poor
falling-down selves and as we put ourselves back
together once again at the table.

This table has been a house in the rain, an umbrella
in the sun.

Wars have begun and ended at this table. It is a place
to hide in the shadow of terror. A place to celebrate
the terrible victory.

We have given birth on this table, and have prepared
our parents for burial here.

At this table we sing with joy, with sorrow.
We pray of suffering and remorse.
We give thanks.

Perhaps the world will end at the kitchen table,
while we are laughing and crying,
eating of the last sweet bite.

—Joy Harjo

CANNED POTATOES. A strange catalyst for a philosophy about food and community, but for me, that's where it all started. I wish I could tell you a story about how learning to cook in an old farmhouse kitchen at my Grandma Duffy's knee inspired and informs my cooking today. But I can't. Don't get me wrong—there were plenty of fantastic meals during my childhood. But looking back, the meal was the price of admission for time spent around the table, not the main focus of the evening.

I spent every Sunday night of my youth at Grandma Duffy's eating overdone beef roast, a sensible vegetable (peas or squash), and little, perfectly round, skinless potatoes cloaked in butter and parsley. Those meals are etched in my mind with indelible ink. I remember how the wool carpet felt under my feet, how I felt so grown-up listening to adult conversation, chasing peas around the plate with my fork, the smell of coffee brewing that signaled the imminent arrival of dessert, and my escape to the den and Mutual of Omaha's *Wild Kingdom*. But those snowy white, parsley-flecked potatoes: they were my favorite.

For many years after Grandma Duffy passed on, I tried to re-create those potatoes. They were entwined with my love for a woman who provided safe harbor to a girl who loved meringues, books, and dogs, and I wanted to taste them again, as a woman and mother. In my quest to replicate them, I tried everything: peeling B-sized red potatoes; whittling large Idaho potatoes down to that perfect, bite-sized potato nugget. I boiled potatoes in seasoned water and in salted water, and sautéed them in butter. My failed attempts spanned many years, and I never got close to the potatoes I ate at her table.

That is, not until a rocky Lake Superior crossing from Duluth to Ontario in our trawler *Talisker* in 2005. Halfway through the journey I was seasick, miserable, and mutinous. Five children wanted breakfast, and I was close to demanding that we turn the boat around. Ted, a good captain and an even better husband, offered to make potatoes. Indifferent, I mumbled, "I just want to go home," and I sat down on the steps near an open window. He handed a plate to me and headed back to the fly-bridge. In my wave-addled state, I mindlessly took a bite. Wait a minute. We didn't have fresh potatoes on board, only canned. And yet here it was: the elusive Grandma Duffy potato. What the hell was going on? How had Ted conjured her potatoes in the middle of the biggest freshwater lake in the world?

Canned potatoes. Did it matter that I had spent years trying to re-create something I could have purchased in aisle six? Did canned potatoes mean my grandma loved me any less? Did the potatoes even matter? Perhaps I had been trying to re-create time spent at her table and not the potatoes all along. On that trip along the northern shores of Lake Superior, I realized that food is a conduit to what I truly treasure: family and friends around our table.

* * *

As a teenager I devoured books, and I particularly loved stories about the English countryside. While most girls were thinking about Guess jeans and Tretorn tennis shoes, I longed for a large stone hearth, a handful of spaniels, an AGA stove, and a farmhouse table. The table of my dreams would see me through a lifetime of dinners, birthday cakes, homework, dogs who sit in chairs (okay, I really had no idea I'd ever own a dog who sat at the table), blueberry pancakes, Monopoly marathons, cribbage games, and friendships forged over plates, forks, and glasses of wine.

Then one early December about fifteen years ago, just after we moved into our home in Woodbury, I spotted the perfect table at Restoration Hardware on Grand Avenue in St. Paul. It was eight feet long, made of planks from a whiskey distillery in England, and it was on sale. The table barely fit in our dining room, and we didn't have enough chairs, but it was exactly what I had dreamed of. We hosted Christmas Eve dinner for my family that year—all seventeen of them.

Our table isn't fancy, but it's well loved. Ted takes a belt sander to it every few years to clean up the stains, dings, and scratches; we rub it down with beeswax, and then it's time to add the patina of living, eating, playing, and studying all over again. Along with many a Christmas dinner, we've eaten bone marrow, oysters, Scotch eggs, porchetta, soufflé, pizza, smoked ribs, corn dogs, and a timpano on its knotty planks. Gathered around it we've celebrated birthdays with Thomas the Tank Engine Train, the Wiggles, skateboards, and pony cakes. It's seen its fair share of glue, glitter, and markers (before I declared the Dougherty home a craft-free zone), and it has withstood little kids wielding forks, Matchbox cars, and Legos. I laid my head upon it and wept when I learned Ted's dad had passed on. We've named babies, dogs, and boats

while seated around this table. It's been the first line of defense for mail, schoolbags, baby seats, laundry, grocery bags, textbooks, and all the miscellaneous items that seem to reproduce around our house. It is a testament to the last fifteen years of our lives, and as the kids grow up and move on, it will be the wooden four-legged tether to our precious history.

The beautiful part of the story told by a family table is that *it goes on*. It goes on to include friends not yet met, partners not yet married, and grand-children not yet conceived. But they are coming, and when they do our table will continue to bear witness to the blessings we are so very fortunate to receive. It's our legacy reimagined as a table.

Acknowledgments

THIS BOOK CAME TO LIFE thanks to a whole cast of characters to whom I owe a multitude of heartfelt thanks and many, many good meals with even better wine.

To Kathy Borkowski and everyone at the Wisconsin Historical Society Press for taking a chance on a first-timer and believing in this book.

To Kate Thompson: your tireless and wise editing ferreted out exactly what I meant to say, often with a lot less repetition! You are a word wizard.

To Demaris Brinton for your gentle persistence and resolute insistence that this book needed to be on the shelves at Apostle Islands Booksellers.

To Sara Ann Sexton for introducing me to Harriet the Spy as a girl, for teaching me that words matter, and for being the voice in my head that reminds me that love and loyalty are the name of the game.

To my mom, Patty Carlin, and my grandma, Pat Duffy, for passing on the importance of the connections made in the kitchen and at the table. The kitchen is home to me, thanks to you.

To Bridget Oporta for always being there. From the beginning when we were partners in catnapping crime to a treasured friend and sister as adults. You mean the world to me.

To Julie Buckles and Charly Ray for your friendship, which started with a second-grade dog-sledding adventure, quiche, and homemade dog treats at Good Thyme and has traversed all sorts of ground: Pagan Dinner Club, tequila in the sugarbush, Bark Bay Slough, LICC, and camping trips that never happened. Life is better with you around our table.

To the family and friends who've passed through our kitchen, sat around our table, and patiently waited for dinner to be served well after 8 P.M.! You've contributed your own flavors and stories to the mix, and this book wouldn't be the same without you.

For Jack, Will, Sadie, Charlie, and Meg. Without you, these stories would not have been written. I thank my lucky stars every day that I am your mom.

Finally, to Ted Dougherty, for approaching me on the 52B University of Minnesota bus all those years ago. Your dad's gift of Anne Morrow Lindbergh's book *A Gift from the Sea* when I was a young woman has proven to be prophetic and so, so very true: "The web is fashioned of love. Yes, but many kinds of love: romantic love at first, then a slow-growing devotion and, playing through these, a constantly rippling companionship. It is made of loyalties, and interdependencies, and shared experiences. It is woven of memories of meetings and conflicts; of triumphs and disappointments." I love you, plain and simple.

Index

Note: Page numbers in **bold** type refer to primary recipe locations.

About the Author

AFTER A SAILING TRIP to Lake Superior and the Apostle Islands, Mary Dougherty transplanted her family of seven plus four dogs from the suburbs of Minneapolis to Bayfield (population 487). She opened and co-ran Good Thyme Restaurant, recognized as one of the top dining experiences in northern Wisconsin, for four years. She went on to create the Cookery Maven blog and Words for Water, a photography project giving voice to people about the importance of fresh water. Founder of the nonprofit Farms Not Factories, she now serves on the board and is a rabble rouser for the Socially Responsible Agricultural Project. You can find her most mornings at the beach with her dogs and most nights in her kitchen cooking for family and friends. She is, as *Edible Magazine* reported in 2012, "the quintessential perfect host."